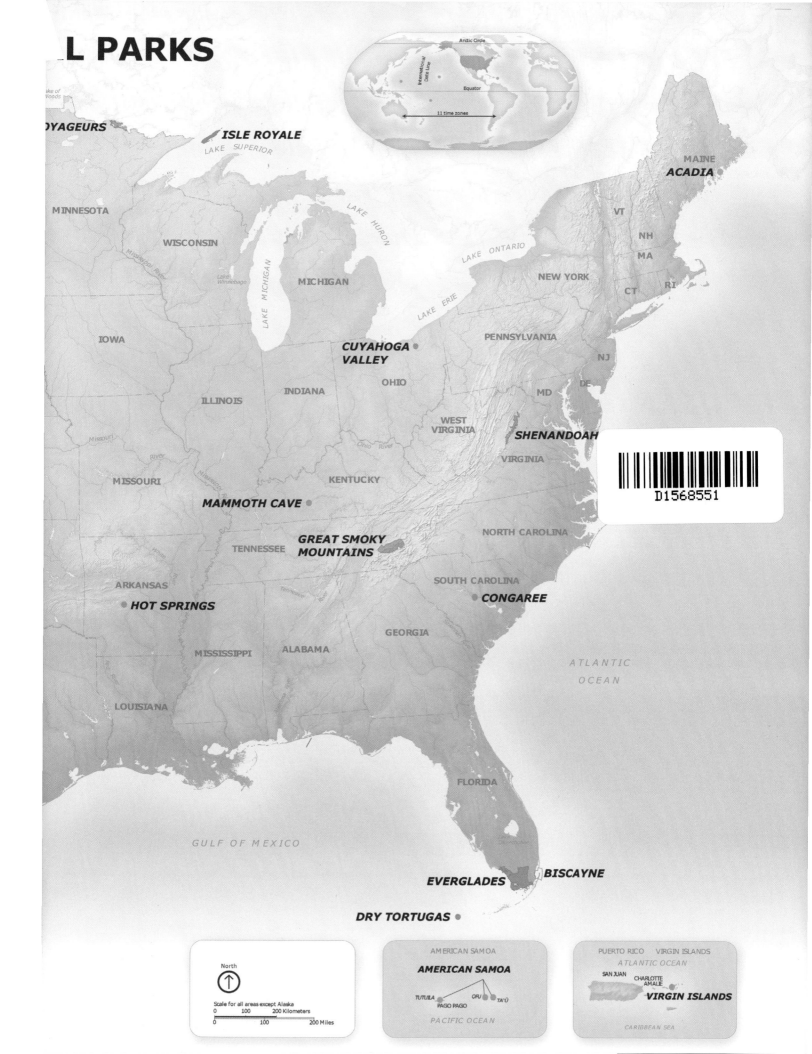

L PARKS

VOYAGEURS

ISLE ROYALE

LAKE SUPERIOR

MINNESOTA

WISCONSIN

MICHIGAN

LAKE HURON

LAKE ONTARIO

LAKE ERIE

MAINE

ACADIA

VT

NH

MA

NEW YORK

CT

RI

IOWA

Lake Winnebago

LAKE MICHIGAN

CUYAHOGA VALLEY

OHIO

PENNSYLVANIA

NJ

INDIANA

ILLINOIS

MD

DE

WEST VIRGINIA

SHENANDOAH

Missouri River

Ohio River

VIRGINIA

MISSOURI

KENTUCKY

MAMMOTH CAVE

NORTH CAROLINA

Mississippi River

TENNESSEE

GREAT SMOKY MOUNTAINS

ARKANSAS

Tennessee River

SOUTH CAROLINA

CONGAREE

HOT SPRINGS

GEORGIA

ATLANTIC OCEAN

MISSISSIPPI

ALABAMA

LOUISIANA

FLORIDA

GULF OF MEXICO

Lake Okeechobee

EVERGLADES

BISCAYNE

DRY TORTUGAS

North

↑

Scale for all areas except Alaska

0   100   200 Kilometers

0   100   200 Miles

AMERICAN SAMOA

AMERICAN SAMOA

TUTUILA

PAGO PAGO

OFU

TA'Ū

PACIFIC OCEAN

PUERTO RICO   VIRGIN ISLANDS

ATLANTIC OCEAN

SAN JUAN

CHARLOTTE AMALIE

VIRGIN ISLANDS

CARIBBEAN SEA

Arctic Circle

International Date Line

Equator

11 time zones

INSPIRED BY THE
NATIONAL PARKS

Their Landscapes and Wildlife in Fabric Perspectives

Schiffer Publishing Ltd
4880 Lower Valley Road • Atglen, PA 19310

Donna Marcinkowski DeSoto

Other Schiffer Books by the Author:

Inspired by the Beatles: An Art Quilt Challenge, ISBN 978-0-7643-4700-9

Other Schiffer Books on Related Subjects:

Yellowstone National Park: Past & Present, Suzanne Silverthorn & I-Ting Chiang, ISBN 978-0-7643-4175-5

Visions: Earth's Elements in Bird and Nature Photography, Kevin T. Karlson, Lloyd Spitalnik & Scott Elowitz, ISBN 978-0-7643-4075-8

American Heroes Quilts, Past & Present, Don Beld, ISBN 978-0-7643-5045-0

Designed by John P. Cheek
Cover design by Brenda McCallum

Type set in Goudy Old Style/Sabon LT Std

ISBN: 978-0-7643-5119-8
Printed in the United States of America

Published by Schiffer Publishing, Ltd.
4880 Lower Valley Road
Atglen, PA 19310
Phone: (610) 593-1777; Fax: (610) 593-2002
E-mail: Info@schifferbooks.com
Web: www.schifferbooks.com

For our complete selection of fine books on this and related subjects, please visit our website at www.schifferbooks.com. You may also write for a free catalog.

Schiffer Publishing's titles are available at special discounts for bulk purchases for sales promotions or premiums. Special editions, including personalized covers, corporate imprints, and excerpts, can be created in large quantities for special needs. For more information, contact the publisher.

We are always looking for people to write books on new and related subjects. If you have an idea for a book, please contact us at proposals@schifferbooks.com.

To Kurt, in thanks for a multitude of blessings he brings to my life.

CONTENTS

FOREWORD

As a little boy, I used to walk along the rocky shore of an island in Biscayne Bay, flipping over rocks and poking at crabs. It was there that I fell in love with the Bay's warm, shallow waters, and all the life they nurtured. When I was seven, my parents were inspired by my twenty-something-year-old brother's hitchhiking journey across the US. Deciding to forego a long-planned trip to Hawaii, instead they purchased a fifteen-foot trailer and a pickup truck. For six weeks our family visited places with names like Bryce, Carlsbad, and Dinosaur. I remember listening to a man in a green and gray uniform talk about the white sands of New Mexico. He was smart. He was funny. I could tell he loved what he did. I decided that I, too, wanted to be a park ranger someday. Just fourteen years later, that dream came true, and not long after that, these two stories had a happy collision: I became a ranger in the national park that protects the majority of Biscayne Bay, my childhood playground.

A ranger's job isn't always what people expect. Yes, I get to be outside more than most, and yes, I get to meet people from all over the world and help them appreciate why the over 400 places protected by me and my coworkers in the National Park Service are worth protecting, and yes, I still enjoy flipping over rocks and poking at crabs. In an electronic age, though, the way people connect with their national parks is changing. Rangers manage websites, write Facebook posts, and work with communities to create a cadre of people who work together to protect these pretty extraordinary places. That said, some things haven't changed . . . like the role artists play in protecting national parks.

In the early 1870s, the renowned landscape photographer William Henry Jackson and painter Thomas Moran were both part of an expedition that explored an area of Wyoming and Montana that native peoples referred to as the "land of the yellow stone." In 1872, President Ulysses S. Grant declared Yellowstone as the world's first national park. The action was due in no small measure to Jackson's stunning photographs and Moran's luminous paintings. These brought the grandeur and majesty of the place to an audience who otherwise could have no comprehension of the area, and made them appreciate a place they had never seen. By so doing, they paid that landscape the ultimate compliment: stewardship.

Nearly 150 years later, artists are still forging connections between the national parks and the people who own and visit them. Photographers and painters have been joined by sculptors, potters, dancers, musicians, and those who take the folk art of quilting to an entirely new level. These are not Grandma's bed coverings! Art quilts are a separate breed. Their creators use fabric and thread, yes, but they do so in a seemingly limitless number of ways. In my twenty-plus years at Biscayne National Park, I have had the great pleasure to work with artists in all kinds of media who are inspired by the parks, and they have given me new ways to look at a place I already love deeply. For that I will be forever grateful.

As the nation celebrates the centennial of the organization that manages the national parks, from enormous Wrangell-St. Elias and Yellowstone to much smaller sites like Walnut Canyon National Monument and Thaddeus Kosciusko National Memorial that recall the early days of an extraordinary experiment called America, it seems very appropriate to celebrate some of the best-known among those parks by hearkening back to the beginnings of an idea that was completely new: protecting a place not for its monetary value, but rather for its spiritual value. Places that pay interest not in dollars, but in experiences that last long after money runs out. Places that are worth protecting for future generations not just by politicians and park rangers, but rather by all those who own them, including artists who believe that their work can and does make a difference in their protection.

History has proven that they are right.

Gary A. Bremen
Park Ranger
Biscayne National Park
July 2015

ACKNOWLEDGMENTS

So many hands, minds, and hearts came together to produce this book. Let's start at the beginning. Thank you to Pete and Nancy Schiffer for another opportunity to make my dream of being a writer come true.

I have enormous appreciation for and gratitude to Sandra Korinchak, senior editor at Schiffer Publishing. In her most capable hands and under her diligent watch, a manuscript was crafted and transformed to become this book.

Thank you to my Mom and Dad, Dolores and Frank Marcinkowski, for opening my eyes to the wonders of America the beautiful, and for my first lessons on the importance of home.

Thank you to my nephew Greg Marcinkowski, for his deep passion for the national parks; this is where the seed for this book began. My friend Barb Hollinger enthusiastically helped to establish plans and parameters for the quilts, and my son Andy suggested the park ranger narratives to accompany the art quilts.

I had an ambitious crew for the photo shoot and I thank you for your time, patience, and expertise: Carey Massimini of Schiffer, and Mary Kerr and Beth Shafer, who have been most generous in every single aspect of being dear friends.

Thank you to my trusty researchers, Bobbie Dewees and Tammy Howell; you were speedy and diligent in your eager assistance.

To these sunbeams, who make a huge difference day to day by being great listeners, positive forces, and calm, smart, and sensible confidants: Norma Fredrickson, Jeanne Coglianese, Nancy Adams, Dottie Dane, Kathye Gillette, Kim Gibson, Carol Younce, and Kerry Faraone, I so appreciate your firm shoulders, gentle words, and warm smiles.

Jennifer Weilbach, once again, my lifeline, through mountains and valleys. Thank you so much for your keen editing skills, sound advice, and for your friendship.

Thank you to Gary Bremen, for your earnest foreword and for your help in reaching above and beyond among your network of rangers, to fill in gaps.

I am also indebted to many key players, without whose help this book wouldn't have happened. Thank you to the rangers and other national park personnel for sharing your knowledge, thoughts, and insights. And thank you to the artists who responded to this challenge to produce your best work to honor the national parks.

Thank you to the hundreds of members of my quilt guild, Quilters Unlimited. I am proud to be a member of this happy, talented, inspiring, and encouraging herd! In particular, Louise Sutara and Betsy Stone, working with you is my pleasure.

Thank you Kurt, Andy, and Aimee for patience, understanding, and joy. Writing, sewing, and spending time with my quilters makes me a better wife, mom, and human being.

Most of all, thanks to God, who put the critters in the forests, leaves on the vines, stars in the heavens, and all of these remarkable people in my life.

INTRODUCTION

What is it about America's national parks that gets us all misty-eyed?

Is it the memories we have of visiting these places when we traveled as backseat passengers of station wagons, driven by our dads?

Is it the memories we made with college friends, setting out to find our own selves, driving Dodge Darts, and armed with not much more than excellent peanut-butter-sandwich-making skills?

Or is it the other memories we cherish, made from road trips with our own children, who rode in the back of our SUVs, while everyone sang along to Raffi?

What happens when you challenge a group of artists to create original fiber art pieces to honor each of the national parks? They come through. They grew misty-eyed, they swooned, some even loved this idea so much they wanted to make two, and soon so many wanted to participate that there was a waiting list. The artists were given a few parameters. They could choose a park, and one of three categories to depict: landscape, flora, or fauna. The landscape quilts could be either vertical, 20 by 44 inches, or horizontal, 44 by 20 inches; the flora and fauna quilts had to be 20 by 20 inches. By disallowing photo transfer, and encouraging original work rather than the use of commercially-available patterns, we challenged participants to dig deep and come up with creative ways of portraying their subjects. As you look through the art quilts on these pages and read the artist statements, you will see how artists are inspired by national parks.

There are some interesting books offering stories of park rangers. One is called *Oh, Ranger,* written in 1928 by Horace Marden Albright and Frank J. Taylor. It contains a quote by Stephen T. Mather, who was the first Director of the National Park Service: "They are a fine, earnest, intelligent, and public-spirited body of men, the rangers. Though small in number, their influence is large. Many and long are the duties heaped upon their shoulders. If a trail is to be blazed, it is 'send a ranger.' If an animal is floundering in the snow, a ranger is sent to pull him out; if a bear is in the hotel, if a fire threatens a forest, if someone is to be saved, it is 'send a ranger.' If a Dude wants to know the why of Nature's ways, if a Sagebrusher is puzzled about a road, his first thought is, 'ask a ranger.' Everything the ranger knows, he will tell you, except about himself."

But what happens when you give park rangers an opportunity to tell their point of view about their vocation, and about the places where they live and work? They come through with a unique perspective. We read their stories, their thoughts and philosophies, on these pages, and the bonus is we have an opportunity to get to know them. They heard about this project, and were eager to provide their insights to accompany this collection of 177 art quilts. They use the word "love" to describe their day jobs, over and over again. It is clear they do what they do, what they love, because they are inspired by national parks.

Like many, I am inspired by nature. In my backyard, a magnolia tree with enormous shiny leaves thrives right next to a frosty-tipped blue spruce. Plumeria and desert roses bloom in pots on the deck in the back. Hummingbirds dart back and forth between their feeders, goldfinch feast on purple coneflowers, and at last a family of bluebirds has joined the menagerie. We see deer, fox, and a new pair of black squirrels. From a praying mantis on the window screen, to the chipmunk on the woodpile, to the fireflies blinking at dusk, I am keenly aware of nature.

We brought a bit of the outdoors in by painting the walls on the inside of our home mineral green. Depending on the time of day, the light shifts between greenish and blue. The hardwood floors are golden oak, and the walls contain paintings and photographs of trees, oceans, mountains, and flowers. A wall quilt with a moose on it hangs in the powder room. Three cheerful pet songbirds live in a corner of the dining room. This is where magic happens, from my dining room table, where I sew or write. It is where I am both distracted and inspired, gazing out the window or catching sight of the oil painting of Mount Rainier . . .

When it's finally vacation time, we leave this home in search of more nature. We travel to Maine and Nova Scotia, looking for moose. We watch for whales, off the coast of California, where the San Andreas Fault meets the edge of the Pacific Ocean, or we look for dolphins in the Atlantic, from the deck of the Crabby Pelican at Sandbridge, Virginia. Other people are enthralled with the Eiffel Tower or Big Ben; while these places and many others are lovely, we can't get our fill of the national parks.

I am fascinated by the interpretations, materials, and techniques the artists chose to portray their subjects. I don't know if painters and potters and musicians and chefs exchange ideas, techniques, and materials as freely, but quilters have a reputation for doing those sorts of things, and we are all the better for it. Along the way of making quilts, we share knowledge, information, and encouragement with one another. I was so intrigued by the spectacular stitching Marisela Rumberg used on her harlequin duck I took a class from her so I could better hone my own free-motion stitching skills. When I looked at how Cindy Grisdela designed her Wrangell-St. Elias mountain landscape, using bits and pieces of little pieced blocks she had left over from other projects to build her mountains, I eagerly joined her class on improvisational piecing so I could learn to see the way she sees.

National parks are special places to visit. They inspire some to a vocation dedicating their whole lives to preserving and protecting the parks. They also inspire artists. America the beautiful, indeed.

I recently came across a Facebook post where someone said that the first time he stood at the edge of the Grand Canyon he heard "Ode to Joy" in his head. It is my hope you will seek out opportunities, near or far, to visit our parks and to become misty-eyed yourself.

If you would like to reach a particular artist in this book, learn the exhibit schedule for these art quilts, or hear about future projects, contact the author by e-mail: dmdesoto4nps@gmail.com.

WHY JOHN MUIR?

The wrought iron bookends with a peace sign on the dresser in my room hold some of my most beloved possessions. Authors include Chaucer, Twain, Bradbury, Michener, Esar, Lamott, and Blume. The thickest volume is titled *Muir: Nature Writings*. These 800+ pages contain a bounty of wisdom by John Muir (1938–1914), also known as the "Father of the National Parks."

Co-founder of the Sierra Club, Muir advocated to save our wilderness long before it was a cool thing to do. Describing a lifetime of experiences in his travels in extraordinary detail, he touched presidents, Congress, law-makers, and millions of ordinary people. His rich descriptions of sunsets, pine trees, waterfalls, grasshoppers, ants, wildflowers, and thunderstorms awaken every one of my senses.

I have sought refuge in Muir's writings during different phases of my life. When I am pensive, yearning for a break from the harried lifestyle that comes from living in the busy suburbs of Washington, DC, if I am not able to physically get away, reading Muir gives me rest and reason to pause. At other times, when I am already at peace, I open the book, and Muir's musings bring me to a blessed frame of mind. Reading the words of John Muir takes me to

a holy place. While writing this book, I revisited Muir's words with a new sense of appreciation.

Although he died more than a hundred years ago, his fervor resounds: Preserve our wilderness! Protect these precious lands! Experience and value nature!

These sentiments repeat again and again in this book you're holding, through the words of those who most intimately live them: park rangers. While I appreciate the foresight of Muir, I am likewise humbled by the dedication of those who spend their time and energy working to take good care of our parks.

Not long ago, I walked on the grounds of the Muir Woods National Monument, just past the Golden Gate Bridge, so near San Francisco. Taking in the verdant leaves on trees and plants, listening to birds calling from enormous trees, breathing in the pleasure of the warm summer day on a most pleasing shady path, I thought of Muir fondly. Time and again, I was reminded of his accounts as I delighted in the National Parks art quilts created for this project, and even more so when I interviewed park rangers.

In celebrating the national parks, it is necessary to honor John Muir. This book wouldn't have been complete otherwise. A John Muir quote begins each chapter.

ACADIA

"Everybody needs beauty as well as bread, places to play in and pray in, where Nature may heal and cheer and give strength to body and soul alike." JOHN MUIR

Located in coastal Maine; 47,000+ acres
Established July 8, 1916
Official NPS website: www.nps.gov/acad
- John D. Rockefeller Jr. donated all of the land to the state of Maine for this national park
- Cadillac Mountain is the tallest mountain along the eastern coast of the US

Wanda Moran
Park Ranger/Division of Interpretation

It's so beautiful here. I love the ocean. I have worked at Acadia for twenty-three years. The ocean, the mountains, the lakes, and the forests are all in one place. Everything is close by and quite accessible. The view from Beech Mountain is my favorite place in the park. It is a moderate trail to hike, so families are able to climb it easily. The view out to the off-lying islands is spectacular. In the fall, my favorite season, visitors hike to the top of the mountain to observe migrating raptors flying over Mount Desert Island. Leaves change color, there are no black flies or mosquitos, and it's not as hot as the summer. It's perfect weather for biking and hiking.

In 2014, Acadia was voted the number one place to visit by *USA Today*, and was also chosen America's favorite national park by *Good Morning America*.

Acadia Meets the Atlantic

Cyndi Zacheis Souder
Annandale, Virginia

I was intimidated by the prospect of trying to depict the power and beauty of Acadia in fiber. With his permission, I enlarged an image of a photo by Ed Elvidge on my design wall and traced the major elements onto paper. During construction, I traced each element onto tissue paper and used these patterns to fussy-cut and create the appliquéd elements.

I've camped at Acadia and seen the force of the ocean and the vastness of the sky. Recreating the water gave me particular heartburn. I used a commercially-available cotton for the light sections and a hand-dyed organza to get the darker areas just right. I quilted the water very densely to give the impression of movement and direction. After all else was done, I added surf and subtle clouds using paint sticks and small stiff brushes.

Water Lily

Audrey Wing Lipps
Reston, Virginia

I find inspiration for my art quilts in the textures and variations of color in nature. The lily ponds of Acadia provided ample examples of both. I am especially drawn to the pads: those broad, sprawling, shiny surfaces provide a backdrop to the spectacular blossoms bursting up into the air. At first glance the pads seemed uniform, but their subtle differences emerged as I lingered and watched the effect of light and shadow play across the surfaces.

My favorite part of creating art quilts is selecting the fabrics. For this quilt, I especially wanted to portray the variations I saw across the pads. I looked for a mixture of textures and colors and auditioned many options along the way. My goal was to choose the ones that brought a sense of movement and light, for though the pads remained still, on the water, nearby grasses swaying with the breeze often made the pads seem to shimmer.

Snowy Owl

Sarah Ann Smith
Hope, Maine

The lightly patterned snowy owl finds perfect camouflage in Maine's soft winter palette. One day I went walking on the snowy blueberry barrens, where the bright red stems barely poked out of the earth and the stone walls formed crests on the ridges. I thought I had missed seeing the rare visitor until I heard a sound behind me as I returned to the car. The owl landed in a lone tree. Quickly and quietly I grabbed the camera and took many pictures. Unsure which composition I preferred, I created this montage with my own dyed sateens.

AMERICAN SAMOA

Located in the South Pacific Ocean, 2,600 miles southwest of Hawaii; 13,500 acres
Established October 31, 1988
Official NPS website: www.nps.gov/npsa
- The only tropical rainforest national park
- Is closer to New Zealand than to the United States

"The universe would be incomplete without man; but it would also be incomplete without the smallest transmicroscopic creature that dwells beyond our conceitful eyes and knowledge." JOHN MUIR

Samuel Ioka Meleisea
Park Ranger

I have worked for American Samoa National Park for almost five years, first as a volunteer. When the Superintendent for the park noticed my presentation skills and scientific research background, he recruited me as a park ranger because they were seeking young, educated Samoans. This park holds special significance to me because my family has land currently within park boundaries that is leased by the National Park of American Samoa. My family heritage is being protected along with the legacy of my culture.

On a typical day, I might be out in the local classroom, teaching students about fruit bats or coral bleaching. Next I might be at the visitor center greeting a school group who came to see the cool exhibits and to watch park films about Samoan culture. I hike with visitors to the Lower Sauna Ridge trail and talk with them about archaeology and how early Samoans survived by depending on nature. Other times I go to the local market where I give out brochures and answer questions and concerns from the public about the park. There is never a dull moment.

My favorite spot in the park would have to be the Saua site on Ta'u Island. This site is believed by many locals to be the birthplace of all Polynesia.

The National Park maintains a trail leading to this site, which is in the boundaries of my village, Fitiuta.

There are only two seasons in American Samoa, the dry and the wet. I prefer the dry season, which is when we can do the most hiking trips. I love seeing people awestruck by the sheer natural beauty contained here. I have a keen fascination with our fruit bats, which are protected by the NPS. They are the only mammal native to American Samoa, and they are active during the day and at night.

A tsunami destroyed the park visitor center and headquarters in Pago Pago in 2009. Although there were a few injuries, thankfully, there were no park casualties. Some employees lost their homes. Two years ago, we had officially recovered from that natural disaster when the park staff moved into its new headquarters and the visitor center was retrofitted with new exhibits.

American Samoa is the only US national park south of the equator; we are located 60 miles east of the International Dateline. The enabling legislation for this park mandates the protection of the Samoan culture.

The park extends throughout three islands. Our birthday is October 31, which makes for a very spooky celebration!

The national parks are America's best idea. No other organization comes close in comparison to the number of years it has served the American people in the name of conservation. American Samoa is a special place. You haven't been to all of the national parks until you visit us!

American Samoa Underwater Landscape

Susan M. Bynum
Falls Church, Virginia

I have always wanted to do an underwater landscape, so I chose American Samoa National Park. On this piece, I depicted black-tipped reef sharks, a moray eel, damselfish, blue starfish, an angelfish, a green sea turtle, and squirrelfish.

Coconut Tree

Dana Brennan Hancock
Chantilly, Virginia

To me, quilts mean caring. Transforming a few yards of fabric into something to wrap up in or contemplate on a wall is a magical thing. I love making a quilt for someone special, anticipating the joy they will have using a quilt I made especially for them. It is a way I give part of myself. The quilts I design always surprise me when they are done. At times, my initial ideas change drastically as the quilts are constructed.

Inspiration for this quilt came from a photo on the National Park Service website. After initial research about the different types of trees in the park, I e-mailed the park and received a quick and friendly response from Pai Aukuso, a ranger there, who confirmed the tree on the website is a coconut tree. As I made the quilt, I imagined the warm sun, sandy beach, and gentle trade winds at American Samoa. While thread painting the coconut tree, a new technique for me, I could see in my mind the wind blowing the fronds back and forth.

Nudibranch
Linda Keithley
Centreville, Virginia

American Samoa consists in large part of the ocean that surrounds the three islands of Tutuila, Ofu, and Tau in the South Pacific Ocean. Because I am a scuba diver and a retired biology teacher, I was very interested in the fauna that was unique to the waters surrounding the park. When I dive, I look for nudibranchs. This one is common in the Samoa Park waters. Nudibranchs are snail-like animals without a shell. They are found on the plants, sponges, and other surfaces on the floor of the ocean. Their appearance varies widely in size (most are more than one inch but less than five inches in length) and color. Nudibranchs are hermaphrodites with solitary lifestyles. When they meet another nudibranch of their species, they mate and then lay eggs close by in a ribbon configuration.

ARCHES

Located in eastern Utah; 76,519 acres
Established April 12, 1929
Official NPS website: www.nps.gov/arch
- Contains over 2,000 sandstone arches
- 43 arches have collapsed since 1977
- Whoever discovers a new natural arch gets to name it

> *"Every pulse beats high, every life cell rejoices, the very rocks seem to thrill with life."* JOHN MUIR

Leslie Kobinsky
Park Volunteer

I studied environmental science in school and I love working with people in the outdoors; this career is a great way to combine those two passions, and this is why I decided to work for the national parks. I have worked here for the 2014–2015 season as a volunteer park ranger.

Arches is the first park I visited in Utah, and it changed my life. This park inspired me to learn how to interpret and protect natural places. Arriving from a state that was both lush and green, I was taught by Arches to appreciate a new kind of beauty in the unforgiving terrain of a desert. The hike up to Delicate Arch was incredibly inspiring, especially when I first caught sight of the arch. I was overwhelmed, as Ed Abbey, author and essayist who advocated environmental issues, would say, with the arch's "heart-breaking beauty." In the desert, the will to survive is an underground pulse that resonates under the sand, in the berries of a juniper tree, and through the tail of a sagebrush lizard. Nowhere else in the world has the heart of this desert.

The two-mile hike to Park Avenue, my favorite in the park, is often overlooked. Most visitors come to see Arches, or one arch in particular. But to me, Park Avenue is absolutely incredible. Skyscrapers of blood red sandstone shoot onwards and upwards into the awe-inspiring views that encompass Arches National Park. When the views and vistas are cloudy from rain or fog, Park Avenue is still just as beautiful, if not more so. Late winter is the best season in the park. There are fewer people, the weather is milder, and it is a perfect time to have an arch all to yourself.

We have a pair of nesting peregrine falcons in the park. Although the species was de-listed from the federal endangered species list in 1999, it is still listed on Utah's state endangered species list. What a special treat it is to see these birds in this park.

In 2016, the National Park Service will celebrate its 100th birthday. The centennial message for the NPS is to go find your park. So get out there. "Your park" isn't limited to national parks. I would love to challenge every person to find some place close by, a place they have never been to, and plan an adventure. Use public land to explore your own backyard. This country is brimming with incredible places; have fun discovering the places closest to you.

Landscape Arch

Etta McFarland
Olive Branch, Mississippi

Arches was an easy choice for me. During the summer of 1999, my family took our travel trailer to Southern Utah on a tour of the national parks. We saw Bryce Canyon, Zion, and were making our way to Arches when the axle broke on the trailer, totaling it. We never got to Arches, so this is my way of visiting. I decided to depict Landscape Arch, the longest of the many natural arch formations in the park.

There were many exacting steps to take this from a photograph to fabric, and none of them could be rushed. Among the many lessons I learned with this project were how to draw an accurate "cartoon" of the picture to work from, the importance of value over color, and the realization that the quilt doesn't have to look exactly like the picture. In fact, it is better when I make it my own.

The arid desert ground of Arches is protected with a life-sustaining soil crust. The symbiotic relationship between plant life and the earth provides a unique biological ecosystem.

The knobby, black soil crust was made from felted wool and painted with ink blocks. Reflective rayon thread, stitched throughout the soil, replicates watery, blue-green algae sifting through the earth. Mossy areas were created with flocked tulle fused to the sandy background. Bitterbrush is cut from ultrasuede; liverwort was assembled with crushed batik fabric, stitched with silk rayon thread, and brushed with iridescent paint sticks. Indian rice grasses were formed from an ombre yarn and topped with rizo glass beads. Appliquéd trapunto rocks are surrounded with chains of hand-sewn aventurine stones.

Bobcat
Luana Rubin
Boulder, Colorado

Almost 50 species of mammals reside in Arches. One of these is the bobcat. Here in Colorado we have the Wild Animal Sanctuary, which rescues wild animals who are kept in captivity as pets, then are surrendered by their owners when the animals become too big or too wild to be kept in the backyard. I love to photograph the wild cats, especially the big cats of the Western USA. This handsome bobcat caught my eye at the Sanctuary, and doing a quilt of the fauna of Arches allowed me to use this photo as inspiration. This piece is a fundraiser for the Wild Animal Sanctuary, and the sale price will be donated to support the bobcats, tigers, lions, wolves, and bears.

BADLANDS

"Who could ever guess that so rough a wilderness should yet be so fine, so full of good things." JOHN MUIR

Ian Knoerl
Interpretive Park Ranger

I have worked at Badlands for six seasons, the first as a volunteer, the next three as a park guide, then as a physical science technician in paleontology, and now as an interpretive park ranger. I accepted my first position as a volunteer because this is a park with rich fossil history, and I liked the idea of explaining fossils and geology to visitors. This park is special to me because of its combination of geologic formations, prairie wildlife, and fossils. There are many fossils here, but no dinosaur fossils. Most of the fossils found are actually mammal fossils from the period after the dinosaurs.

Located in southwest South Dakota; 244,000 acres
Established January 25, 1939
Official NPS website: www.nps.gov/badl
- Two visitors discovered a large backbone sticking out of the ground near the Conata Picnic Area in 1993
- Fieldwork for the next ten years yielded more than 10,000 fossilized bones for study

Badlands is one of the birthplaces of the science of paleontology.

The place I like best is on the Sheep Mountain Table. From that spot, I can look across and see miles of spectacular scenery. I like the bison. They are truly impressive with their shaggy coats and immense size; it's really cool. They are Ice Age survivors.

Winter is my favorite season. I like how the park looks under a layer of snow. This is an enjoyable place to work. I get to answer lots of visitor questions about the park, and depending on the day, I give walks and talks at one of the park trails, present an evening program in the amphitheater, and work on fossils in the fossil prep lab in the visitor center. The one thing that stays constant is that I get to educate visitors about the park.

Sunset Over the Badlands

Linda M. Moore
Annandale, Virginia

In June 1985, our family embarked on a cross-country camping trip. We traveled 8,500 miles in thirty-two days. We made a goal to visit national parks and monuments. Our time at Badlands National Park was a hot day. I was pregnant and my feet were swollen. I would like to visit again when we can do some hiking. The area was beautiful, as were all of the parks we visited. My quilt was inspired by one of the photographs that I took on that trip.

Snow on the Mountain

Jane LaGree Allingham
Lake Mary, Florida

Snow on the mountain, *Euphorbia marginata*, is found from the Badlands south to Texas. It blooms from July to September. Its contrast of green and white foliage against small white flowers is accented with yellow to gold centers. Although the plant can be grown as ornamental, in the open it is considered weedy and it can cause sickness when eaten by cattle. The milky substance appearing when the plant is picked causes dermatitis.

Of all of the images I found of this plant, the most inspiring was posted by Eileen Horn on the Great Plains Nature Center website. I thank her and the Center for their work to conserve the Great Plains national resource.

Pronghorn
Susanne Miller Jones
Potomac Falls, Virginia

Pronghorn Pete was inspired by a cross-country trip my husband and I took when we were quite young, to celebrate our third wedding anniversary. While going through Petrified Forest, we were stopped by a traffic jam of pronghorns. Todd was fascinated. Later in the same trip we went through Badlands and experienced firsthand the desolate landscape. The pronghorns we saw were so lively, I loved the idea of putting them against the backdrop of the starkness of the Badlands. I truly enjoyed making Pronghorn Pete come to life by layering the fabrics. He took on a personality of his own, right down to the look in his eyes.

BIG BEND

Located in southwest Texas; 801,163 acres
Established June 20, 1935
Official NPS website: www.nps.gov/bibe
- The Rio Grande River traverses the park
- More than 175 species of butterflies have been documented here

"Along the river, over the hills, in the ground, in the sky, spring work is going on with joyful enthusiasm, new life, new beauty, unfolding, unrolling in glorious exuberant extravagance." JOHN MUIR

David Elkowitz
Chief of Interpretation

I came to work at Big Bend because of a lifelong interest in conservation. I have been here for twelve years as the Chief of Interpretation, and three years prior to that as an interpreter. This park is special to me for lots of reasons. We have the best terrestrial diversity in the lower forty-eight, awesome cultural diversity, proximity to Mexico, and remote beauty and wilderness.

My work here is varied. I am busy with partners one day, concessions the next, provide a program to park visitors, work with park staff, and also help out with a special project like the centennial.

I have several favorite places within the park. For instance, there is Marufo Vega Trail and the east side of the park in the wintertime. I love the remoteness, the wilderness, and the views of Mexico; all are truly wild. In winter, the high country mountains of the Chisos provide excellent hiking and views. My favorite season here is spring, due to the bird migration. Early May is when the height of migration for birds occurs. The number of bird species inhabiting here is second to none, within the national parks.

Most people don't know we have the darkest night skies in the lower forty-eight. We also have the greatest Cretaceous period dinosaur diversity of all of the national parks. We have fifty-six species of reptiles, leading the national parks in diversity. We have some truly rare and unique reptile species. I once found a large male mountain lion on a trail I was hiking. He sat on the side of the trail, and I was able to view, photograph, and enjoy this symbol of wildness up close. It was remarkable.

The national parks are important to our country because they protect our natural and cultural heritage. They are symbols and reminders of our past, and they present opportunities for learning, for experiencing wilderness, and they will provide outdoor recreation for the future. They also help preserve species diversity and offer wild places for the soul.

Casa Grande: Through the Window

Barbara E. Kauffman
Waterford, Virginia

To me, Big Bend is about sweeping vistas that seemingly go on forever: dramatic, stark beauty. Desert mountains form an ever-changing kaleidoscope of color as harsh afternoon light softens to dusk, the epitome of purple mountain majesties. Thirty years of living in the Southwest are indelibly imprinted on my mind and in my heart. Big Bend National Park is one of my favorite places on Earth. It is remote and forbidding and hushed. The land gathers you in, and takes root in your soul. This piece celebrates the bold, rugged, radiant splendor of Big Bend. The park is truly a national treasure.

My quilt is based on the photograph *Outside the Window* by Gordon Wolford, which was used with permission.

Catclaw Mimosa

Elaine Kelly
Reston, Virginia

Insignificant from more than a foot or two away, the catclaw mimosa is marvelous up close. It is a fluffy, pale pink ball made up of countless filament-like petals. But if you get that close, you risk being snagged by the namesake thorns.

In my quilt, I wanted to focus on the flower, capturing its exuberance and making it larger than life. My core challenge was to figure out how to translate that beauty and energy into cloth. How to make the centers? Foundation piecing with tulle for the negative space eventually did the trick. How to give the flowers dimension? Dozens of different fabrics, eight different silks for the flower tips, and hand appliqué with silk thread all contributed.

Nature encourages me to go slow and look closely. Representing this little flower in fabric was a rewarding journey requiring me to find my own path.

Javelina

Claire Alison Josiak
Calgary, Alberta, Canada

Javelinas, also called peccaries, are pig-like creatures with prickly personalities. They drink water when it is available, but can survive on succulents in times of drought. As the day heats up, javelinas find shelter in shaded areas such as caves and dense brush. They feed more in the cooler months and less during hotter temperatures, when they prefer to rest. They spread out from each other while feeding, but during the night they huddle in groups of about fourteen for warmth and protection. They live for approximately seven years in the wild.

I lived in Texas for three years and had an opportunity to visit Big Bend. Although our visit was hair-raising because our vehicle had bad tires on an unusually hot day that was 115°F, we had a wonderful experience floating down the Rio Grande and hiking in the desert.

My inspiration for this modern piece with traditional elements came from the Louisiana artist George Rodrigue who created the *Blue Dog* paintings. I wanted my javelina to be of strong design and bold color; fierce but whimsical, to make him lovable. Big Bend javelinas have small eyes, rough hair, and a "collar" around their shoulders. Their hides were used to make brushes in the 1800s; what could be better than to make an image of a javelina with a brush cut hairstyle?!

"Through the afternoon all the way down to the sunset the day grows in beauty." JOHN MUIR

Located in southern Florida; 172,971 acres
Established October 18, 1968
Official NPS website: www.nps.gov/bisc
- 95% of this park is water
- Home to at least sixteen federally endangered species, and two federally endangered plants

Gary Bremen
Park Ranger

I was born and reared in South Florida. Initially, I wanted to visit national parks different than what I was used to. I came to a strong realization that my connections to this place as a child gave me a greater sense of purpose. I began working at Biscayne National Park in 1989 as a seasonal ranger, and joined the park's permanent staff in 1995.

It's tough to say what my favorite season is here. December through March is busy with lots of activity from visits by winter-weary northerners. Summer's calm days are best for visiting the park's vibrant reefs and gin-clear waters. Fall, though, often has the best of both worlds, as long as a tropical storm system is not passing through. Visitors tend to be thoughtful and interested and they have a passion for the national parks just like I do. I think Biscayne would be a very strong contender if there were a "Best View from a Visitor Center Desk" contest! Just outside are miles of moody waters: sometimes turquoise and calm, sometimes gray and choppy with white waves biting like teeth at an angry black sky.

Unfortunately, my work doesn't get me out into our 173,000 acres very much. My job frequently involves planning and partnerships and creating new ways for people to connect with a place they cannot easily visit, due to lack of a boat. This park is the result of a grassroots effort by a small committed group of people. The incredible natural resources of this land were threatened by imminent development. I love the human history best. For 10,000 years, varied people ranging from those shipwrecked, to pioneers, millionaires, presidents, pineapple farmers, Cuban rafters and even freedom-seekers on the Underground Railroad, have spent time at Biscayne.

I love the little things, and the little-known things of this park. Nearly 600 species of fish have been documented: this number is larger than all of the birds, reptiles, amphibians, mammals, and fish combined at places like Yellowstone or Yosemite. Upside-down jellies rest on the bottom in the shallows of Jones Lagoon, tentacles towards the sky, exposing their symbiotic algae to the sun. The mangrove rivulus is the only self-fertilizing hermaphroditic vertebrate in the world, and they hang out right outside my window! Magnificent frigatebirds soar effortlessly along the shore, staying in the air for days at a time using feathers whose total weight exceeds that of their bones. Shall I go on?

A memorable highlight was 2010's National Geographic BioBlitz, a twenty-four-hour count of as many living species as possible inside park boundaries. Over 200 people helped, and the excitement of together documenting 1,027 species, including one completely new to science, was absolutely palpable.

National parks reflect the very best and the very worst about America. They have the ability to make our hearts soar with pride in the beauty of the land and the accomplishments of her people, but they can also make us cry for what was lost and at the stories of how inhumanely people have treated one another. The real value of the national parks isn't about any one location. It isn't about Biscayne or Grand Canyon or Martin Luther King Jr.'s home or the Statue of Liberty. It is how these 400-plus places mesh together to tell a much bigger story. It is this synergy that I love most.

Matt Johnson
Public Information Officer

Soak up the sun, listen to the wind and the songs of wild birds, immerse yourself in a halo of light, treasure moments of silence, and enjoy the company of others, human and animal, all of which and more may be experienced in Biscayne National Park.

Elizabeth Strom
Park Ranger

I have always been grateful for the best job in the world. I work in a national treasure. My office is the ocean. My coworkers are mermaids and pirates. I have saltwater in my veins. I share the ocean's wonders with park visitors. And I get to raise the most beautiful flag on July 4, the celebration of our great nation's Independence Day.

Biscayne Landscape
Dianne Harris Thomas
Fairfax, Virginia

Since being near any salt water makes me happy, I was delighted at the opportunity to depict shoreline scenery for this project. This national park is unusual because most of it is underwater. The only land included are several small, uninhabited islands, many completely covered by low-lying plant life. Yet from this remote and beautiful place, you can easily see the Miami skyline.

Twice this year we went to Florida's east coast to visit family. We spent many hours swimming and snorkeling. Once a late-summer thunderstorm produced a gigantic black cloud that hovered over us as evening darkened into night. The powerful, frightening, fascinating cloud inspired my portrayal of Biscayne, showing the waters in sunny and stormy weather, and during a sunset.

Beach Morning Glory

Julia L. Renken
Fairfax, Virginia

Ipomoea pes-caprae (also known as railroad vine, goat's foot vine, and beach morning glory) is a plant found along seashores from the Atlantic coast of Georgia through Biscayne National Park, around the Gulf Coast to Padre Island Seashore in Texas and beyond, into Mexico. This vine is often used in beach restoration and stabilization. It grows rapidly and can send out "tracks" more than 100 feet long. My knowledge of this plant came about during my younger daughter's study of the plant's characteristics for her dissertation in Aeolian geomorphology.

These flowers usually open late in the evening. By mid-afternoon the flowers have faded. The flowers I show here are representational of the full flower seen in the morning, my favorite time of the day.

The background quilting represents the tracks of vines across the dunes. The leaves, flowers, vine, and stems were hand appliquéd and then quilted, to enhance their characteristics. A hand-quilted design depicts waves of water approaching the shore, in the border of this piece. I was inspired by Ruth McDowell's flower foundation piecing method.

Queen Triggerfish

Linda T. Cooper
Burke, Virginia

One of life's best treats is snorkeling with tropical fish. While I've never been swimming with queen triggerfish, I love their colors and beauty. I made an amusing version of this fish, a triggerfish with a tiara-topped cowboy hat, pink boots, and a spear gun at the ready. But in the end, I opted to put that one on the reverse side of this piece (detail shown at right).

BLACK CANYON OF THE GUNNISON

"*Every morning, rising from the death of sleep, the happy plants and all our fellow animal creatures great and small, and even the rocks, seemed to be shouting, 'Awake, awake, rejoice, rejoice, come love us and join in our song. Come! Come!'*" JOHN MUIR

Located in western Colorado; 30,750 acres

Established March 2, 1933

Official NPS website: www.gov/bica

- Parts of the gorge receive only 33 minutes of sunlight per day
- The Painted Wall within the park is the highest cliff in Colorado

Nick Myers
Park Ranger

I dreamt of being a ranger since I was eight years old, when I attended a ranger-led program at Wind Cave National Park. I was struck with the thrill and excitement of leading these kinds of programs. I have been here since June 2014. This is the best position I've ever held in the National Park Service. We do everything from staffing the park visitor center to conducting overnight backcountry patrols. Black Canyon is the best and every day here is memorable. It is a place of extremes, yet is so approachable.

I love Dragon Point, for the amazing views of the river, canyon and sunsets. During autumn, the temperatures are perfect and oak leaves are golden brown. Most people don't realize how powerful the river is. The Gunnison River roars through the canyon; this amazing power continues to down cut the canyon walls. Our bobcats are rarely seen, but in the wintertime, their tracks are evident. I love knowing that big predators are in the park, just as they have been for centuries.

The national parks are an integral part of the American character. They are the symbol of freedom, space, history, and the future.

Birds' Eye View of the Black Gunnison

Kerry Faraone
Purcellville, Virginia

I fly once a year to California over the magnificent gorges of the southwest United States. Because of the erosion of the earth, water against rock, I find this area, as well as the Grand Canyon, fascinating.

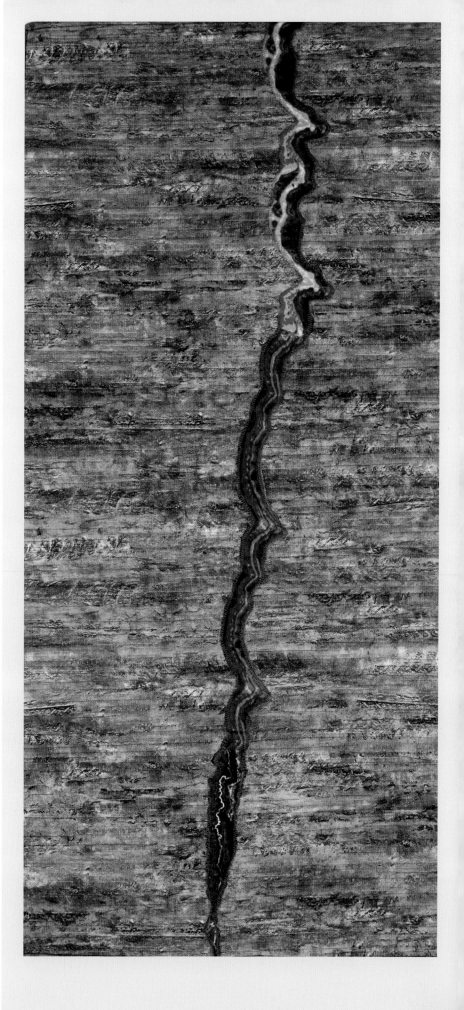

Twisted Juniper Tree

Nicki Allen
Springfield, Virginia

I have always had a strong desire to make things, and over time, I have come to appreciate the vast possibilities that quilting offers as an art form. The process of making an art quilt taps into my brain in a way nothing else does. I love the challenge of designing the quilt, picking the fabrics, and executing a plan.

When I begin a new piece, I let it simmer for a while. Sometimes I know exactly what I want to create, but more often, it takes quite a bit of time to envision the completed project. It is that vision that drives my process.

Gunnison Sage Grouse
Jeanie Sakrison Velarde
Cordova, Tennessee

While researching national park flora and fauna and trying to decide what to do for this challenge, I came across this bird and fell in love with him, as soon as I stopped laughing. I learned that he is on the endangered list, so I envisioned him out there, dancing his heart out, trying desperately to attract a lady grouse. Then they could make baby grouses and get off the endangered list! The whole time I worked on him, all I could hear in my head was "Oh, oh, oh, oh, stayin' alive, stayin' alive." Of course, there just had to be a disco ball.

Located in southwestern Utah; 35,835 acres
Established February 25, 1928
Official NPS website: www.nps.gov/brca
- Famous for geological formations called hoodoos
- On a clear day visibility can exceed 100 miles

*"How wonderful the power of its beauty!
Gazing awe-stricken,
I might have left everything for it."* JOHN MUIR

Jan Stock
Revenue and Fee Business Manager

I have worked at Bryce Canyon for twenty-nine years in five different capacities: interpretive park ranger, Superintendent's secretary, ranger activities assistant, interpretive park ranger, and revenue and fee business manager. I decided to work for the NPS because of my love for nature and the outdoors. It is important to me that we protect special places for future generations. I also have a desire to interact with interesting people from all over the world. Bryce is special for its beautiful and bizarre rock formations, which are ridiculously picturesque. Bryce has unparalleled vistas. On a clear day, you can easily see over a hundred miles across the Grand Staircase-Escalante National Monument. Since I am not a fan of large cities, I appreciate the fact that this park is situated in a wonderfully remote and largely unpopulated section of the western US.

Working at Bryce Canyon National Park is enjoyable and rewarding, as well as challenging and frustrating. From March through November, long lines of cars full of people come through the entrance stations to spend a few hours or a few days visiting the park. We receive about 1.5 million visitors a year, and every year our visitation increases. The free Bryce Canyon shuttle operates May through September to alleviate some of the traffic in the park, since there is

only one parking space for every four cars. We collect in excess of $3 million per year from our visitors at the entrance stations. Most of this money is used for a variety of projects and services that directly benefit the visitor (trail maintenance, interpretive programs, custodial services, new restroom construction, visitor center museum remodel, for example). Despite this funding, our backlog of critical infrastructure repairs and improvements continues to grow. It's a problem common to most National Park Service sites. Bryce Canyon is understaffed. We have the smallest Interpretation Division of any NPS site on the Colorado plateau, despite having the fourth largest visitation.

Hiking the strenuous eight-mile-long Fairyland Loop Trail is one of my favorite things to do. This trail is jam-packed with hoodoos, arches, and fins, and is one of the lesser-used trails in the park. There is plenty of opportunity for solitude and reflection there. Winter is probably the most beautiful and serene time of year to experience Bryce. The contrast of red rock, white snow, and stunning blue skies will take your breath away. It is the quietest time of year in terms of visitors, so it enables us at the park to recharge our batteries after many months of hectic and stressful activity, leading up to winter.

Probably the most memorable thing to happen to me, personally, is that I met the love of my life in the park, a fellow interpretive park ranger, many years ago! This turns out to be not surprising, and from what

I hear, not uncommon; when people with common interests and a shared passion for their agency's mission are working together, it makes perfect sense that they fall in love and marry.

National parks protect what is important to our nation, whether it's beautiful things like mountains, lakes, and forests, or not-so-beautiful things like Japanese concentration camps, blood-stained Civil War battlefields, or schools that tell the story of segregation. Every one of the 407 National Park Service sites preserves part of who we are and what makes our country special. In my opinion, if we were to lose these irreplaceable locations, each and every one of us would lose a piece of ourselves. We need these national parks more than they need us.

Hoodoos at Twilight
Kathryn Gray
Manassas, Virginia

My friend and I entered the Bryce Canyon just before dusk and drove to the nearest overlook. As the night crept in, the valley floor deepened into shadow, but the sky, although darkening, stayed bright blue. The moon shone across the valley of hoodoos as the sun, while setting, turned their tops to gold. The Native Americans thought this was a holy place, and the hoodoos were believed to be the bodies of ancestors, frozen in place in this world.

Hood's Phlox

Diane Dresdner
Chantilly, Virginia

While hiking, I was captured by the beauty and strength of this cheerful little flower growing out among the rocks. Observing the striking contrasts in color and texture, I was stopped in my tracks. This quilt is inspired by a photo I took and by the emotions I felt on that day.

I was able to use several techniques I have learned. This is an idea I've wanted to try for some time: I cropped a portion of the photo I took and enlarged it to make my pattern. The rock fabric is cotton I dyed myself. The fabrics were first fused and then sewn into place. I painted portions of the quilt and used trapunto on several flowers. I used needlepoint yarn and a French knot technique for the flower centers. After quilting, I then painted additional areas.

I have enjoyed many national and state parks. I am always enriched, awed, and renewed by the beauty, variety, and surprises of nature. I am proud to be a part of this project and hope we spread and increase a love and joy of nature.

Prairie Dog

Joyce Badanes
Bluemont, Virginia

I love the national parks, and am overjoyed to participate in this centennial celebration. It was the perfect opportunity to make my quilt art mean something more than just art fun. Traveling and experiencing art in nature is my most potent inspiration. Translating these experiences to an art quilt is the greatest fun I have in my life. My work is first of all intuitive. I draw on what I have learned from many well-known artists. I readjust and envision anew if necessary, rather than being self-critical.

For this project, I researched on the web and looked through my own pictures of Bryce Canyon. I settled on a lone prairie dog, standing as a sentry among the blades of grass. First I drew a small picture, enlarged it, then copied the enlarged version on a piece of freezer paper. Selecting fabric from my stash, I figured out how to begin. I found a piece of fabric I had dyed and then selected more greens and many browns. I used some of what I had recently learned from Ruth McDowell, as I cut up the drawing and ironed each part onto a piece of brown fabric. These "puzzle" pieces were put together on the green background and then sewn down. Last came the grass, which I cut and placed randomly. I am continually learning and love the process. This is what gives me spiritual joy and a reason to live fully and productively, even in my advanced years.

CANYONLANDS

"God himself seems to do his best here." JOHN MUIR

Located in southeastern Utah; 337,000+ acres
Established September 12, 1964
Official NPS website: www.nps.gov/cany
- Canyons and buttes were carved here by the Colorado River
- 4,000 year-old pictographs can be seen in the Horseshoe Canyon area

Kathryn Colestock-Burke
Seasonal Park Ranger

I grew up in a camping family. All eight of us would pack ourselves into the 1964 VW van and explore our country each summer. Every national park was a new delight, and as a young girl I dogged the park rangers mercilessly because I wanted to learn everything I possibly could from them. They were superheroes to me! Since I never met a female ranger in the 1960s, I didn't know I could become one, and I took another career path. Forty years later I had the privilege of becoming a summer park ranger through the federal grant called "Teacher to Ranger to Teacher," which opened the door to an exhilarating, life-changing job in the wilderness. I am in my seventh season at Canyonlands, working in the Division of Interpretation to assist visitors in making intellectual and emotional connections with the park during their stay.

Canyonlands, the largest national park in Utah, is centered around the confluence of two mighty rivers of the West: the Colorado and the Green. The erosive power of these waters, and of every drop of rain falling on this area, has carved intricate canyons and labyrinths of sandstone into the Utah desert. Canyonlands embodies so much I am passionate about: supreme beauty, deep wilderness, solitude and silence, and a rich cultural history. To find all of this in one singular place has been a blessing. In addition, the struggle for life is played out daily in this harsh desert environment. Our plants and animals must find a way to endure heat, drought, low humidity, and scarcity, earning my profound respect for the remarkable adaptations that ensure their survival.

There is a spot that captures my heart each time I hike to it, at the end of the White Rim Overlook trail. Almost a mile out on a long spit of land, with sheer cliff edges dropping 1,300 feet, I can sit under an overhanging rock and savor rare shade while being amazed at the 301-degree view unfolding before me. These canyons, carved by the Colorado River and every drop of water running into it, glow iron-red in the sunset. The 12,000-foot La Sal Mountains reflect the day's last rays. February is spectacular in the park, when visitation is lower and the weather is crisp and sunny. Red rock is a stunning complement to white snow. Occasionally we experience temperature inversions that push clouds below the canyon rims, creating postcard-worthy views that leave me in awe even after many years here.

I love putting on my uniform each morning, the green trousers with sharp creases, the gray shirt with shiny gold badge and nameplate, and the embossed brown belt with pinecones on it. I lace up my favorite boots, grab my flat hat, and head into the park to do a variety of things, depending on my shift. I might give a geology talk at the cliff edge, or hike a trail to remove graffiti. I staff the entrance booth to welcome visitors and collect entrance fees. Some part of each day is spent in the visitor center assisting folks in planning their day in the park, creating just the right itinerary for their time, abilities, and interests. Every day is different. I may be needed for a SAR (Search and Rescue), tumbleweed-pulling, driving a coworker to town for emergency medical evaluation, or speaking to a school group. Here in the northern district of the park, we live in a small wilderness "neighborhood" with seven houses and about eighteen staff members. It is 45 minutes to the nearest grocery store, mechanic, bank, restaurant, gas station, or doctor. One learns to plan ahead

and to do without. In our off hours, since we have no TV signal, we read, cook, hike, play musical instruments, write, gather for potlucks, watch the stars, or just embrace solitude.

Most people don't know how hard our flora and fauna work to survive in the desert. With fewer than ten inches of precipitation annually, and humidity typically below 20 percent most months of the year, organisms must be creative in meeting their water needs. We have kangaroo rats that never take a drink their entire lives, instead absorbing moisture from the seeds they eat. There are juniper trees here that can self-prune during drought, sacrificing a limb or two to save themselves. Desert bighorn sheep can lose up to 10 percent of their body weight between visits to their water sources. My favorite flora is the sacred datura, and I am partial to the desert bighorn sheep. I have written blog posts about these at www.arches.wordpress.com/2011/07/02/ogling-the-datura and www.arches.wordpress.com/2013/04/17/the-bighorn-and-i.

The park is filled to overflowing with memorable events. Some are dramatic, like all-night moonless searches that end with finding a lost hiker. Some are tender: marriage proposals in a carefully selected place filled with meaning. Still others are imbued with deep meaning that may not become evident for years: a child's first encounter with a lizard, which leads to a path of becoming a herpetologist, or a hiker's sense of discovery at finding not just new places but new abilities within himself or herself.

National parks exist in America because visionary people saw the treasures in our landscape and deemed it our responsibility as a people to preserve them unimpaired for future generations. Their foresight created the opportunity for our children's children to be able to have the same transcendent experiences, the same connections with the natural world, the same opportunities to visit places essentially unchanged for millennia. As in the nineteenth century, vigilance is required to protect the dwindling amount of wilderness that remains. These parks belong to each one of us who call ourselves Americans. They are our birthright. They protect fragile landscapes and cultural wonders, and preserve bits of history that might otherwise go untold.

Grand View Point

Tina Lewis
Parker, Colorado

I am a Utahan and was delighted to recognize the natural beauty of Canyonlands with my version of this overlook. The end panel of my landscape depicts the Holy Ghost panel in the Great Gallery of Horseshoe Canyon. This unique rock art is called Barrier Canyon Style (BCS).

Barrier Canyon rock art includes pictographs, painted figures, and petroglyphs: figures etched in rock with a sharp stone. The Great Gallery containing twenty anthropomorphic figures is 200 feet long and fifteen feet high, and is the best preserved BCS rock art, suggested to be between 2,000 and 4,000 years old. Another claim

to fame for Horseshoe Canyon is that Butch Cassidy hid there in the late 1800s.

For this quilt, I used a couple of new techniques. Terry Chase introduced me to discharging fabric (using dark fabric in bleach solution to take some of the color out of the fabric). I used this technique to achieve the color for a couple of canyon walls. She also helped me to dye the fabric. I enjoyed adding dimension to the rocks. I worked from a panoramic photo my husband took when we visited Canyonlands in 2013.

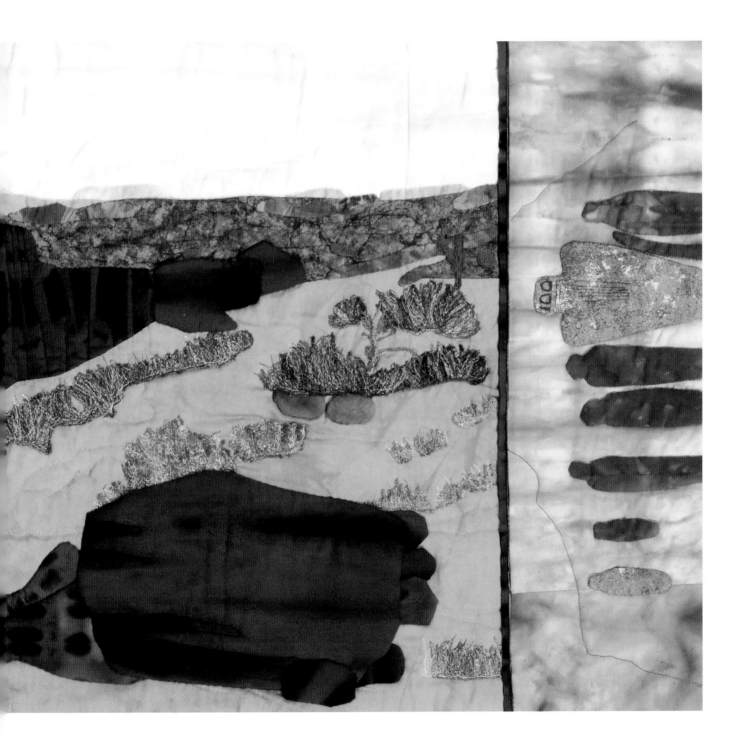

Monkey Flower

Linda M. Moore
Annandale, Virginia

What an interesting wildflower the monkey flower is! In some species, you can actually see the face of a monkey in the flower. A reddish variety grows at Canyonlands.

This quilt was fun to design. I used free-motion appliqué and hand embroidery techniques.

Tiger Salamander

Bobbie Dewees
Springfield, Virginia

I am not normally a fan of slimy amphibians, but I was up to the challenge of creating a salamander from Canyonlands National Park. There are many varieties of salamanders found in all of the states but the tiger salamander is the only one found in Canyonlands National Park.

Mine was made using raw edge appliqué, machine piecing, and machine quilting.

CAPITOL REEF

Located in south-central Utah; 241,921 acres
Established August 2, 1937
Official NPS website: www.nps.gov/care
♥ Named for a line of Navajo Sandstone
formation domes and cliffs that resemble
the US Capitol building

"Every architectural invention of man has been anticipated, and far more, in this grandest of God's terrestrial cities." JOHN MUIR

Cindy Micheli
Park Ranger, Interpretation

I grew up an outdoorsy gal on the East Coast and worked in Manhattan for a major publishing company for many years, after earning my degree in writing and literature. The urban environment felt like a poor fit for me. I found my place, the red rock country of the Colorado plateau, during an accidental trip out West, and I schemed to make it my home. A broad knowledge base, variety of customer service skills, and a sincere desire to share our nation's places of great beauty with others enabled me to obtain seasonal employment with the National Park Service. I never looked back, working my way from park to park, one opportunity at a time, until coming to Capitol Reef. I have worked here for twenty years, hired as a park ranger in the Division of Interpretation with corollary duties as an Education Outreach Specialist. I also am the Division's Volunteer Coordinator, managing several astronomy volunteers, Geoscientists-in-the-Park interns, adult volunteers and student groups, as well as college and university internship students throughout the year.

Every day at work here is different. Or maybe I should say, every minute is different. I come to work and help get the visitor center ready for our public. I pull the weather forecast from the Internet, check on current road conditions, and post the day's ranger activities. During the morning, I check the Internet for information requests and answer questions about the park online. I may be scheduled to give a geology talk or coach an intern's talk, or open up the one-room historic Fruita schoolhouse for a few hours, so visitors can come inside. I sometimes eat lunch with our administrative staff to share stories about what is happening in the park. In the afternoons, I may get out to hike a popular spot in the park and answer visitors' questions. More likely, I will be helping to staff the information desk in the visitor center, working on timesheets and statistical reports, or writing notes for an intern or volunteer's talk review or putting together a letter of reference. During the school year, I travel to a dozen local schools, within a one hundred mile radius of the visitor center, and give presentations to fourth graders on the park's natural and cultural resources that tie into Utah core curriculum standards. I also travel to nearby towns to provide talks to Scouts, 4-H groups and historical societies. I write brochures, articles, press releases, funding proposals, and exhibit text, to name a few.

Capitol Reef was created at the same time as Arches, Canyonlands, Zion, and Bryce Canyon. But due to its remote and rugged nature, it remained isolated with only dirt roads until 1962. This park's natural beauty, ecosystem diversity, and cultural history rival those of any neighboring park. Our atmosphere is relaxed, unhurried, and almost conversational. There is no press of millions of visitors, elbowing their way through to a jammed parking lot overlook at this park! At least, not yet.

The Sulphur Creek route is my favorite part of the park. This six-mile hike drops into a narrow canyon fed by a mountain creek. I always see wildlife on this route—snakes, birds, deer, butterflies—as I drop down ledges, crisscross the stream, and wonder at modest waterfalls that have acquired deeply incised layers of sedimentary rock over millions of years.

I enjoy fall the best. Summer heat and monsoonal thunderstorms have ended by then, and the air is crisp and clear. The morning air has a bite to it, but the days remain bright and warm. Schoolchildren visit the park on field trips, and fall seems to be the season when I look beyond the towering red cliffs into the cerulean blue sky, and I can see infinity.

Our park just applied for International Dark Sky status. My favorite thing about Capitol Reef's isolation is the lack of ambient light at night. With no major population center for hundreds of miles around, the stargazing is phenomenal! A full moon truly illuminates the landscape. A moonless night sky is carpeted with starlight and stardust.

I am partial to the diminutive canyon wren, for its subtle yet extraordinary beauty. Its stout little body has a long slender bill on one end, and is balanced by a thin elegant tail on the other. Its feathers show every shade of brown in the most delicate and minute pattern. The canyon wren's song steals my heart! Its trill is a liquid decrescendo of fast-paced notes, slowing as they travel down through the octave, ending with a squawk known as a kiss.

As for memorable events, in mid-January, 1997, we had a snowfall of two feet, and two subsequent nights were minus two degrees. For a park with an average low of twenty-two degrees (our coldest month is December), and less than ten inches of precipitation a year, this was incredible. Another exciting event was in the summer of 2014, when the Utah Symphony Orchestra toured Utah's "Mighty 5" national parks, and the members performed at our campground amphitheater.

Each park tells a part of the story of who we are as Americans. Whether they tell about our wild animals and courageous landscapes, or about our history and our culture, they embody the various facets of our collective identity, from our most noble heroics in pursuit of freedom, to our traditions of slavery, to our expansive confidence in subjugating a continent, to our precise, exact, and scientific efforts to keep a species from extinction. National parks integrate the elements of these stories; they are these things themselves: not pictures, not videos, not books, but the actual real deal. At Capitol Reef, it's the flash flood grinding tons of water, silt and rock through narrow canyons, widening and deepening cuts in the landscape. It's the wild cougar, leaping upon a deer and bringing it down to satisfy its hunger and that of its growing cubs. It's the hand-me-down textbooks lying open-faced on the desks in the 1896 pioneer schoolhouse. It's the twang of rural fiddle music playing in the shade of an historic settler's homestead. It's the impression of prehistoric track ways, made in mud hundreds of millions of years ago, and exposed for a child's wonder.

Our mission is a delicate one: to preserve these places and yet make them available to the millions who come to learn, to see, to recreate, and to refresh and restore the spirit. Treat these treasures gently, but visit your national parks, as many of them as you can. Immerse yourself in the stories each park has to tell. Discover how our history has shaped you, and allow it to inspire how you shape our future.

Fruita View

Sylvia Borschel Lewis
Ephraim, Utah

As a native Utahan, I have always been a big supporter of the national parks in my state. I was thrilled to portray Capitol Reef, which is nearest to where I live. Although it is one of the lesser-known parks in Utah, it is every bit as beautiful as the more popular parks. I wanted to capture the feeling of the strata in the rocky landscape. Using a photograph from the National Park Service website for inspiration, I was able to mimic the line of the horizon to guide me in filling in my mosaic.

Claret Cup

Stacy Rausch
Arlington, Virginia

To make this quilt, I started by hand painting the background fabric. Using photos as inspiration, I drew the flower and cactus shapes freehand. I appliquéd pieces using fusible interfacing. After all of the shapes were ironed in place, I hand embroidered the details and machine quilted the sky.

Broad-Tailed Hummingbirds
Nancy B. Adams
Annandale, Virginia

I appreciate the birds of the national parks as well as the exciting large mammals. This tiny, 3½-inch bird has a distinctive wide tail. I was as accurate as possible with my Capitol Reef hummingbirds, but the flowers are my own version of trumpet vines.

Located in southeast New Mexico; 46,800 acres
Established October 25, 1923
Official NPS website: www.nps.gov/cave
🛡 The 120 caves of this park were not carved out by running water and streams; sulfuric acid dissolved the limestone along the cave rocks to form the caverns

> *"The dead and the living, rocks and hearts alike, awake and sing the new-old song of creation."* JOHN MUIR

Steve Behrns
Park Guide

I can still remember the bat flight program when I visited this park as a seven-year-old kid. The memory of dark creatures flapping and flying out of the cave is a vivid photograph in my mind! I have a deep love for the multiple species of bats at Carlsbad. They often get a bad rap, thanks to many superstitions, which cloud the reality of how important their survival is to our existence. They pollinate and protect many plants, which sustain the lives of countless humans and animals. I am at Carlsbad because I have a great love for wildlife.

Life here can be busy and hectic. There is an incredible amount of work and collaboration to make everything happen. We have a great team so we are able to provide an amazing experience for our visitors.

The natural entrance and amphitheater is an iconic gateway to Carlsbad Caverns, and it is my favorite spot. There is so much mystery and wonder hiding below this arched hole in the Chihuahuan Desert. Many people are unaware that the park is a part of the Chihuahuan Desert, the wettest and most biologically diverse of four major desert zones in the United States. (The other zones include the Mojave, Sonoran, and Great Basin.)

My favorite season is autumn. Temperatures are pleasant and are a welcome break from the nonstop 100-degree marathon of summer. Autumn is also a great time to visit our nearby sister park, Guadalupe Mountains National Park, where maple and oaks explode into autumn colors.

The national park system is a belief and practice that is held in high regard around the world. The thing that drives our mission is a passion to preserve, protect, and learn about our last great resources and wonders. Guarding these places not only protects the balance of nature, but ensures our wellbeing. From cancer research to economic growth and countless recreational opportunities, the worth of these national park treasures we safeguard and share with the world is inestimable.

Carlsbad Caverns and public lands around the nation need your help. When you visit these places, you create memories and invaluable experiences for your family as well as yourself.

Totem Pole, Domes and a Doll's Theater

Joan M. Gifford
Gainesville, Virginia

I acquired a love for wild caves while crawling around in them in Pennsylvania and West Virginia. I first saw Carlsbad Caverns about forty-five years ago and it is still as awe-inspiring today as it was then.

My quilt is a celebration of the vastness and variety of formations in the caverns. In nature, some stalactites are so small, and some stalagmites are gigantic, yet it all comes together beautifully.

The spelunker on my quilt, with his hardhat, carbide lamp, and climbing rope, looks at everything in total awe. He is thinking about where he will explore next.

Sunflower

Amalia Parra Morusiewicz
Mitchellville, Maryland

Once having lived in this land of enchantment, I know the sun plays a key role. Deep in the Carlsbad Caverns, wonders exist in the dark. This park offers more than just the interior of the caves. Outside, bright sunflowers welcome bright sunshine.

This piece is whole cloth quilted using silk, paint, and embroidery.

Mexican Free-Tailed Bat

Joyce Bounds
Annandale, Virginia

My quilt displays the Mexican bats found at Carlsbad Caverns. The primary viewing of these bats occurs when they swarm at sunset; thousands of bats leave the caves simultaneously. The silhouettes of the bats create a stunning visual display as they move in various formations. Even though I last saw the bats in 1972, I distinctly remember them rushing from the caverns into the sunset sky.

CHANNEL ISLANDS

Located in coastal Southern California; 249,561 acres
Established March 5, 1980 (first designated a national monument in 1938)
Official NPS website: www.nps.gov/chis
⬦ The oldest human remains in North America, dating to 13,000 BCE, were discovered on Santa Rosa Island

"Lowly, gentle fellow mortals, enjoying God's sunshine, and doing the best they can in getting a living." JOHN MUIR

Ian Williams
Park Ranger

I had wonderful times camping in the national parks when I was growing up. I always admired the people who worked in the parks. I wanted to do more than visit these places; I wanted to be a part of them. I have worked for twenty-three years now as a ranger on San Miguel Island.

The Channel Islands are so isolated from civilization and yet there are big cities only a few dozen miles away. The solitude one can find on the islands is enchanting. Moreover, the ecological solitude of the islands has allowed endemic species to develop here, just as Darwin discovered in the Galapagos.

Half of the park is land, and half is water. I'm not sure if any other park is as evenly balanced. I love being in the unseen underwater part of the park. On a sunny day in clear water, there is no place as ethereal as looking up towards the surface through the golden columns of giant kelp, backlit in the sunlight, as fish swim all around. Many people who live in Southern California have never seen the Channel Islands, and they don't realize this place is a national park.

One animal stands out above all at the Channel Islands: whales. When you see a whale spout or breach out on the ocean, it always stops you in your tracks. There are some species, like blue whales, the largest whales on Earth, that I never thought I would get to see in my lifetime, but they are right here, and I see them around the Islands every year. The most memorable happening has been the recovery of species of animals that have flirted with extinction. During the history of this park, brown pelicans, peregrine falcons and island foxes have all made amazing recoveries. There are many species in other places that may never recover, due to habitat loss and ecosystem disturbance. Here in the Channel Islands we have the opportunity to restore and preserve a crucial place for these rare animals. The Islands are an intact habitat for many species.

In 2016, the National Park Service celebrates its centennial. What we celebrate, however, is not just 100 years of an agency serving the pubic. We also celebrate the fact that 100 years ago, a private citizen named Stephen Mather cared enough about the national parks that he put his personal effort and fortune into seeing they were properly managed and cared for. When the NPS was created, he became its first Director. It has taken both private and public stewardship to create and protect the parks. The NPS centennial celebrates both.

Channel Islands Landscape
Corinne Sovey
Austin, Texas

I have always loved the water and I grew up on the coast of Southern California. I have such fond memories of sunsets on the West Coast. I decided to make my quilt very graphic, with bright colors to boldly represent the unique vitality of the islands. I used a variety of techniques to communicate the islands, including something called matchstick quilting (dense machine stitching in straight lines) in various thread colors to communicate depth in the water. This quilt takes me back to my childhood, and making it made me realize I need a vacation!

Giant Kelp

Lisa B. Ellis
Fairfax, Virginia

This piece represents the rich beauty of the undersea world in the Channel Islands. When the sunrays penetrate the shallow waters, the kelp leaves appear translucent. Also present in the kelp are the garibaldis; they are the bright orange fish inhabiting the area.

Island Night Lizard

Eileen Doughty
Vienna, Virginia

On Santa Barbara Island, in the Channel Islands, lives this curious little creature. Despite its name, it is most active mid-day, and not at all at night. It gives birth to live young, unlike most other reptiles, which lay eggs. Island night lizards grow slowly and can live to age twenty-five. Also unusual is that their color and pattern is highly variable: mottled, plain, blotched, striped, broken striped, or oscillated. While considered a threatened species, due to habitat alteration in the park and predation by alien species, the island night lizard is not likely to become extinct. What a sadness it would be, if this intriguing little animal were not part of our world.

This whole cloth piece was created using inks, fabric markers, colored pencils, and threads.

CONGAREE

"Love for song-birds, with their sweet human voices, appears to be more common and unfailing than love for flowers." JOHN MUIR

Located in central South Carolina; almost 27,000 acres
Established: October 18, 1976
Official NPS website: www.nps.gov/cong
- One of the highest temperate deciduous forest canopies remaining in the world
- Many trees in the park have Spanish moss growing on them

Jon Manchester
Park Ranger, Interpretation

I have been an interpretive ranger working at Congaree National Park since October 2013. I enjoy sharing the American story with people, and NPS sites allow me to share many stories that are amazing. Whether those stories are about our cultural heritage or the magnificent natural wonders that numerous parks contain, each one is special. I love to see the looks on visitors' faces when they learn something they didn't know before. It is priceless.

There are many things to do here at Congaree. As a park ranger, I might get out on the boardwalk and rove, seeing the people out enjoying their national park. I answer questions and point out unique things that not every visitor gets to experience. I might lead a canoe tour on some days, and get visitors out on Cedar Creek, taking them deeper into the wilderness, away from where any people are. I also spend a great deal of time at the visitor center, helping visitors to get oriented and answering their questions. Through numerous interactions, I hope I have been able to inspire those who visit Congaree to want to become stewards of the world around them and see it with different eyes.

I am a birder, and Congaree is a fantastic place to see all sorts of avian life year round. From winter residents and spring migrants, to summer residents and those passing through on their way south in the fall, I have witnessed the progression of life through these animals. One can tell when the seasons are about to change, just by who flies into the park at different times of the year. I do not have one bird in particular that is my favorite, but I have developed an affinity for the yellow-billed cuckoo. These birds are prevalent, and one can hear them all the time. But seeing these birds is especially hard, as they are elusive, staying high up in the canopy of trees and remaining very still. It took me forever to actually see one; when I do, it is a special treat.

I love to hike on the Oakridge Trail. It is more

remote than other trails: quiet and peaceful. There are enormous trees that have established themselves on this slight rise of land in the floodplain that makes up much of the park. Here you can really experience the Congaree wilderness and escape from the noise and busyness of the city, only twenty minutes away.

I would have to say my favorite season is spring. The return of life to the forest is a fantastic sight to watch. Where once the forest was gray and drab, with bare trees, you begin to see the faint hints to green of leaves, and the red buds of the red maple begin to emerge. And then, with one good rain and a warm day, it all begins to burst forth in color, with the trees leafing out, and the flowers blossoming. It is absolutely beautiful.

Congaree is not really a swamp, though it has been called that for many years. It is in fact a floodplain forest, and the last of its kind. Where once forests of enormous bald cypress and other bottomland trees grew to enormous sizes and dominated the lowlands along many rivers throughout the Southeast, now only Congaree remains as the sole representative of a true old-growth bottomland hardwood forest. Here is where you can get a glimpse of what this section of the country looked like prior to its "discovery" by Europeans.

Congaree is the first park to be created totally through the efforts of citizen action. Harry Hampton, whom the visitor center is named after, began introducing people to the wonders of Congaree. They started to see it not as land owned by a timber company, but as a unique place worth saving and protecting for future generations. The movement grew and the people let their voices be heard, and through their efforts, they were able to secure the protection of Congaree in 1976 as a national monument. It is one of the only parks created by an effort like this.

National parks protect our heritage, both cultural and natural. Without national parks, many of these magnificent natural wonders would have been destroyed by those looking for resources, or by development. Some of our most important historic sites would either have been covered over and made into housing developments, or would have become just another tourist stop with silly souvenirs, instead of places where people can make deeper, more meaningful connections to what these places mean to us as a nation.

For 100 years the National Park Service has preserved the natural and cultural beauty and heritage of our nation. The stories told at the over 400 sites are not always happy stories, but they are important to building understanding. Our parks help us to better understand where we have been. More importantly, they help us to see where we are going.

Elevated Boardwalk

Karen R. Wolfson
Chantilly, Virginia

I started learning about Congaree by looking at the park's official website. Next I did a general online search for photos people had posted of their own vacations. I learned everyone is impressed with the boardwalk.

To make this piece, first I cut a sheet of paper to the size needed for the quilt. I drew a wide horizontal line for the boardwalk. Next I drew lines for the cyprus tree trunks and triangles for their knobby knees. By folding the paper in half along the boardwalk, I could trace the

mirror image for the reflections in the water. I cut up and used my sketch as the pattern to paper-piece, sewing the fabrics right onto my original sketch. Where I was able, I used similar fabrics for the trees and their reflections, but since I only use scraps I didn't always have enough of a fabric to do both top and bottom. It makes the reflection look more like a reflection, so I'm happy with the results. And I can't wait to visit someday to see Congaree in real life.

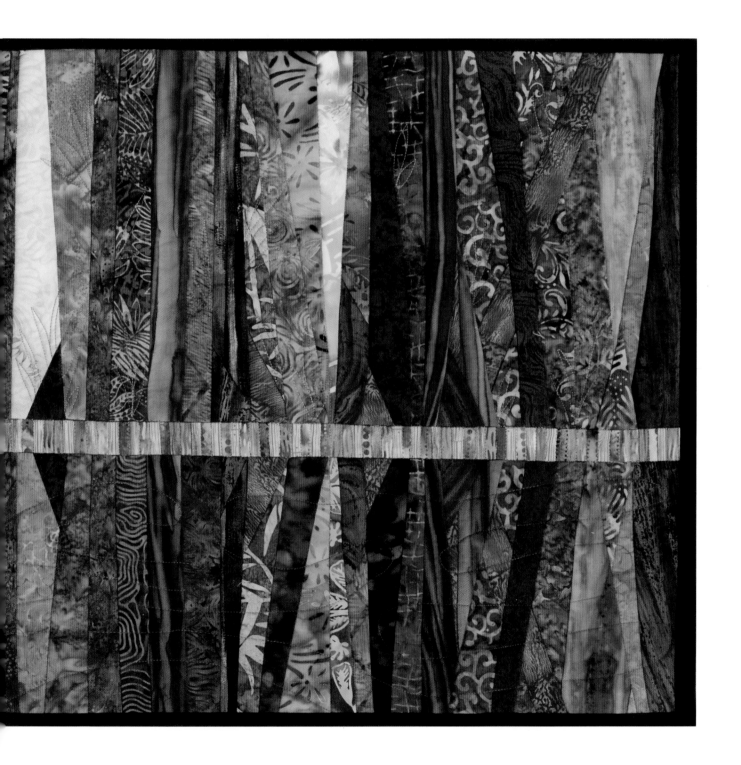

Bald Cypress Tree
Marjorie Dolling Curia
Annandale, Virginia

The bald cypress trees in Congaree are very unusual. Not only do they grow to 100 to 120 feet high and at least three to six feet in diameter, but the bases of the trees are usually much bigger around than the rest of the trees, like elongated pyramids. The bark has thick, ropey ridges and furrows.

The feature bald cypresses are known for is their "knees," a special kind of root. They grow from horizontal roots just below the surface and protrude upward from the ground or water. Since bald cypresses often grow in swampy conditions, it is thought that the function of the knees is to transport air to drowned roots underground. They also might help to anchor the tree.

I enjoy portraying trees in my art quilts. Inge Rappe drew the original artwork on which I based this quilt.

I feel very privileged to have the opportunity to participate in this project. I spent many hours reading information and looking at images of Congaree National Park. Since it's a less well-known park, there is not as much information available as for the more famous parks. I fancy that I might have an opportunity someday to add to the awareness of the park's importance as a wealth of information about many aspects of ancient Earth. How wonderful to discover one of the birds making its summer habitat in the deep forests of the park is the summer tanager.

CRATER LAKE

"How sweet and keen the air!" JOHN MUIR

Matt Daniel
Park Ranger, Interpretation

I began working with the National Park Service as an intern at New River Gorge National River, which was very close to the town I grew up in. While working there, I quickly realized how much more I was learning about the place I had spent most of my life in. That was appealing to me. I have been a ranger here for fourteen months. Crater Lake is so special because I'm not sure if there is another place on Earth that combines such a deep, pure lake with sheer surrounding cliffs and a violent volcanic past.

Located in southern Oregon; 183,224 acres
Established May 22, 1902
Official NPS website: www.nps.gov/crla
⬥ Formed 7,700 years ago when Mount Mazama erupted; centuries of rain and snow filled the caldera and formed Crater Lake, the deepest lake in the US at 1,946 feet

A typical day involves telling visitors from all over the world about the geologic history of Mount Mazama, and about Crater Lake's unusual features. This is told on a boat tour on the lake, trolley tour around the rim, or at the Rim visitor center. Ninety-three percent of the park is old growth forest. The lake itself is without a doubt the centerpiece of the park and the main reason people visit, but the lake is only a small portion of Crater Lake National Park.

In the evening time, the light on Dutton Cliff, Crater Lake, and the Phantom Ship makes for a pretty spectacular view, which is why I would say my favorite place is Discovery Point. We have eight months of winter with an average of forty-three feet of snow. I like summertime best.

I enjoy birds. Elevations in the park range from 4,000 feet to 8,929 feet. These elevations offer diverse habitats, presenting birders with many opportunities to observe a wide variety of bird life.

The eruption of Mount Mazama was 100 times the size of Mount Saint Helens's 1980 eruption. It led to the collapse of the volcano, leaving behind a caldera that has since filled with water. Crater Lake is the ninth deepest lake on our planet. There are 408 individual national park units that work together to tell America's story and connect us to our history, our environment, ourselves, and each other. They are worth protecting because national parks offer opportunities to discover how our individual lives connect to the larger society and the world around us. National parks protect the last, nearly intact ecosystems where natural processes function. This makes national parks invaluable for scientific discovery and education.

TJ Thorne
Artist-in-Residence Photographer

The Pacific Northwest, and in particular, Oregon, have my heart. I found myself as a person and overcame struggles on the ridges, in the waters, and amongst the trees in this state. Crater Lake is one of the more amazing spots I've seen in Oregon. The immense size of the lake and the realization of the cataclysmic event that caused it really put me into my place in this universe. It makes me feel so small in this universe and span of time, but the beauty of it all fills my heart and makes it feel the biggest in the world. It's a juxtaposition that results in wonder, and gratitude. Add in the fact that I can be there in a short drive and it's easy to see why I love this place. I spent two weeks in early October 2014 living in and photographing the park.

I love the top of Hillman Peak. It gives the highest view of the lake on the rim and a direct view of Wizard Island, which is my favorite aspect of the park. This results in being able to view the lake more as a cauldron and volcano rather than just a large lake.

I was determined to capture a special panorama shot as my third image during my Artist-in-Residency appointment, from the very top of Hillman Peak. No matter how busy the park had gotten, I always found myself alone up there, and seemingly alone in the whole park. It's by far one of the best and least visited views of the lake.

My two-week stay was dominated by clear blue skies. While the weather was beautiful for swinging in a hammock, relaxing, and taking in the view, it left me unfulfilled in terms of my photographic desires. Time and time again I made the hike to the top of Hillman Peak with my gear (including camping gear because I never knew if I was going to spend the night there) and got shut down by any kind of less than desirable light or conditions. I'm not complaining. I mean, how could I complain about getting to watch sunset after sunset from this vantage? The fact that I had two whole weeks to do as I pleased, away from responsibilities, in a place as magical as Crater Lake is something I will always be extremely grateful for. This experience would have never happened if I didn't have the support of my friends and family, the encouragement from the photography community, and of course the honor of being selected by the National Park Service to be one of four artists brought into the program. I'm a pretty lucky guy sometimes.

But that's not to say there wasn't frustration. I was, after all, expected to produce art during my stay. I had never had expectations around my art put upon me until then. Not only did I want to produce art that fell in line with the program's focus, but I also wanted to produce pieces that originated more from my love for photography and nature: something personal to me and something I could use to convey the wonder and appreciation I feel for life in nature.

That brings me back to this particular night. I made the steep climb to the top of Hillman Peak for the eighth time, with not a cloud in sight in my shooting direction. My expectations for a shot I would like were pretty low. But I got there early enough to relax. I let the sweat dry from my brow, felt the breeze blow through my shirt, and witnessed the shadows falling across the lake once again. A wall of clouds was to the west, so the chance of nice light hitting the rim was nonexistent. There I waited, frequently looking back to see if there would be a break in that wall of clouds, but it was not to be. The minutes passed and those clouds drew closer. Soon enough, they were at my back and I watched them spill over the rim into the caldera. I was enveloped in the quickly moving atmosphere and it was the first time during my residency that everything I had been waiting for bubbled to the surface. Maybe not the exact light I was expecting, but what I wanted was to feel alive: not relaxed, but alive. All of those frustrations were whisked away by the elements and I shot away with a huge smile on my face. The excitement of living filled me to the brim and I couldn't help but let out a "wooooooo!" at the top of my lungs. The sound echoed through the park and I have no doubt that if you were standing on the rim of Crater Lake on October 14, 2014 you heard it. Up there in the fog, with my camera and my goosebumps, I was the only man on Earth.

This shot epitomizes so much about my personal experience during the residency; it's the crown jewel of my stay. I hope that you can experience a little of what I felt when you look at this photo: www.tj thornephotography.com/Galleries/Recent-Work/i -QJwd9jJ/A.

My favorite season at Crater Lake is winter. The rocky, alpine environment, mixed with the softness of the snow on the trees and the contrast of the white snow with the blue waters adds a whole other level of beauty.

One of my favorite things in the park are the whitebark pines. The beautiful gnarled wood has withstood thousands of years of extreme weather on the rim. Sadly, more than half of them are either dead or dying, due to climate change and infestation by the pine beetle, which has made it to higher elevations because of the rising temperatures. These trees lack the defense mechanisms to withstand the attacks and it's very apparent as you drive through the park.

With growing populations and industries, national parks are at risk of being destroyed. I've already seen some of my favorite natural areas being affected. Places that have remained fairly untouched by man are now disappearing or being defaced with graffiti. I love that people are getting out and seeing the natural beauty that surrounds us, but I wish we were all a little more educated on ways to keep the parks around longer so that future generations have a place to see, appreciate, and maybe help to overcome their challenges.

Cascades of Snow in Summer
Carole A. Nicholas
Oakton, Virginia

Inspiration for my work often comes from remembered images of specific places I have visited, particular patterns observed, feelings and emotions evoked by a certain experience, and the interplay of light and color. Nature always provides an endless source of references to interpret in fabric and thread. There are unlimited possibilities in this process of creating. Each artist's vision and techniques are uniquely different.

Crater Lake has been described by author Roger A. Vincent as "the clearest, deepest, bluest, most breathtakingly beautiful lake in the United States." Yes, when I first saw it, the unforgettable cobalt blue color took my breath away. I remember feeling a sense of wonder, seeing the intense deep blue water, with cascades of snow around the caldera, even though it was summer. High on the crater's rim only the hardiest trees survive, bent and twisted from the ferocious winds and harsh conditions. At lower elevations, much of the park is a forest of hemlocks, firs, and ponderosa pines, which in places give rise to canyons or meadows clothed in wildflowers in summer.

I enjoy the challenge of transforming images in my mind into a quilt, simplifying complex elements to create something tangible. In this landscape I have included Wizard Island, a miniature volcano more than 755 feet high. I used textile paint to add depth to the landscape and give the appearance of steep cliffs around the crater; layers of tulle suggest reflection and shadows. Angular piecing made a dramatic sky, and hand embroidery produced dimensional features on the tree stump and the flowering plants clinging to the rocky ground.

Western Columbine

Tammy Howell
Salem, Oregon

Nature inspires me. No two flowers are alike. Grass is not crayon green but contains a kaleidoscope of shades and colors. I quilt with many fabrics, numerous shades to imitate the beauty and complexity of nature. I make decisions in quilts based on color. Why use one red, when a columbine has six different reds? Or sixteen? Traditional watercolor quilts are made using squares. I designed my watercolor columbine using triangles. With the smaller pieces, I was able to shade more delicately and use more colors. In studying the columbine, I discovered flowers are not made with chunks of the same color. The colors change as the light and shade changes around the flower.

I used heat-set crystals for the first time in this project. I love how they add the sparkle of dew to my columbine. Using color on a design board, without a set pattern, was a challenge. I enjoyed exploring new techniques and the complexities of a beautiful flower in this project.

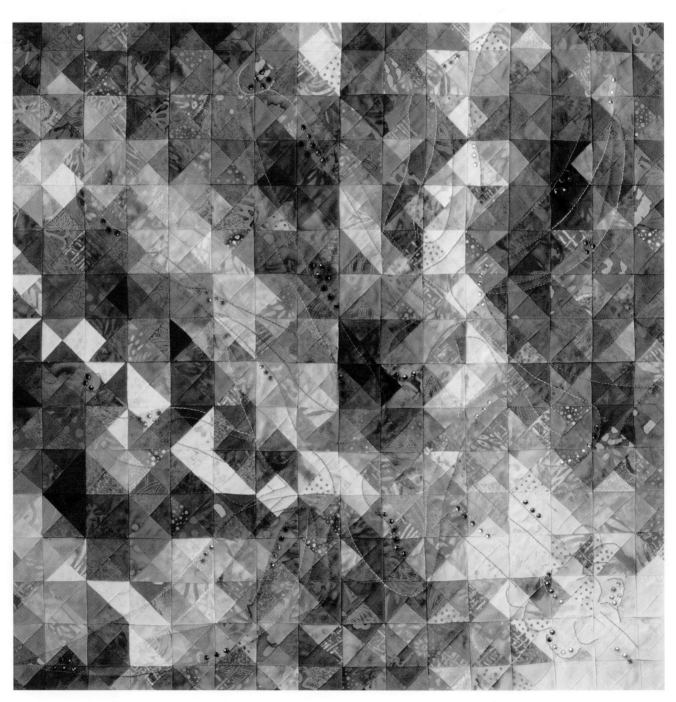

Stellar's Jay

Judith Newman
Fairfax, Virginia

I saw my first Stellar's jay on a visit to Lake Tahoe. I was intrigued by how different it was to the eastern blue jays I am familiar with. Later, when I visited Crater Lake with my son Jay, I saw a Stellar's jay overlooking the lake, just as shown in my quilt.

To make this quilt I used fabric that I dyed and hand painted with markers and alcohol. Snippets of fabric were fused onto the background. Special thanks to Karen Wolfson for helping with drawing the design, and to Kyoko Yamamura who did the machine quilting.

CUYAHOGA VALLEY

Located in northeast Ohio; 33,000 acres
Established June 26, 1975
Official NPS website: www.nps.gov/cuva
- *Cuyahoga* is a Mohawk word meaning crooked river
- The 308-mile-long Ohio and Erie canal, dug by hand in the early 1800s, runs through the park

"Innumerable green and yellow buds were peeping and smiling everywhere." JOHN MUIR

Rebecca Jones Macko
Interpretive Park Ranger

I had the "misfortune" of being dragged to state and national parks every summer by my parents. Each year we went at least twice to the Smokies. In college, I randomly applied for a job with the NPS, but with no luck. After trying my hand at teaching, I applied once more to Mammoth Cave and the Smokies. Mammoth Cave took a risk hiring me. Within two weeks, I knew what I wanted to do for the rest of my life. It was like falling into a net: a moment of a-ha! I met my husband here and my son took his first steps in this park. People get engaged, married, celebrated, and remembered here. How cool is that? I have worked at Cuhahoga for more than fifteen years now.

Is there is such a thing as a "typical day"? Today I had a meeting, pre-hiked a trail for a program this weekend, planned Facebook postings, answered e-mail, and talked to visitors about programs. Tomorrow, I will research another upcoming program. This weekend I have a six-mile hike and will spend seven hours at an information desk in a visitor center.

I still visit national parks, only now I drag my son along. Of all the parks I visit, though, Cuyahoga Valley has one of the most diverse program offerings. Not everyone is able to get

to Wrangell-St. Elias, but Cuyahoga Valley introduces national themes to an urban audience.

My favorite spot is probably along the Columbia Run, just off the Buckeye Trail. Or maybe it's along Sagamore Creek, also just off the Buckeye Trail. Both spots have steep ravines with a meandering stream at the bottom. There are places to sit amongst hemlocks and quietly listen to the water below. I love the smells, the crisp air, and the colors of fall. That said, I rejoice each spring when the area finally greens up after another "Cleveland" winter.

The muddy ditch running the length of Cuyahoga Valley was a national player in the economic development of America. The Ohio and Erie Canal opened up the West, but also sent valuable resources east to crowded and hungry places like New York City.

I have an affinity for the cardinal and the fox. Year-round residents, I love their bright colors. The red fox is being out-competed by the coyote, though.

National parks tell our story. Independence Hall speaks to the good we can strive for, while battlefield sites tell the lengths we will go to in order to defend our beliefs. We remember sacrifices: Gettysburg, Valley Forge, the American Samoas. We celebrate our success: Edison NHS, George Washington Carver, Rosie the Riveter. And for those in large urban areas, we are the green space and buffer: Gateway, Golden Gate, Indiana Dunes, Cuyahoga Valley.

A Day at Beaver Marsh

Julie B. Riggles
Annandale, Virginia

At the Beaver Marsh website, I found its history to be very interesting, and I also saw beautiful pictures of the marsh. After I got a feel for the area, I sketched a layout of my ideas, complete with dead trees, water, and animals. I tried to capture the calm and space of the marsh, along with some of the resident animals. I enjoyed making this quilt and hope this project will bring attention to supporting our national parks in the future.

Beth Wiesner
Woodbridge, Virginia

Most of my quilts celebrate flowers, but they also contain elements of all the things I love: family, friends, nature, and books. Two books I read as a child have inspired most of my quilts, in particular: a field guide to wildflowers that I carried with me everywhere, and a children's novel that introduced me to quilting. I think of my quilts as a way to tell the stories of my life. While the viewer might see a common milkweed, I see a three-generation family bike ride, a walk with an old friend, and an unfortunate incident involving my sister, my mother, and some milkweed fluff.

My quilts begin with research. I want to learn as much as I can so I use books, magazines, and Internet searches to get started. I take walks in the woods or gardens, looking for and photographing wildflowers. I think of my flowers as whimsical botanical illustrations. They are hand appliquéd and scrappy; this quilt has fifty-four different fabrics and 150 buttons. I love color, texture, and variety, which might be inspirational or it might be because I can't make decisions!

Blue Heron

Susan J. Sladek
Fairfax, Virginia

I remember a boating party on the Cuyahoga River when I was in college in 1970. At one point, someone threw a match into the river and a flame appeared. The river and its marshes had become a toxic dumping ground, so badly polluting the river that even the blue heron stopped coming.

In 1974, the Cuyahoga was named a National Recreation Area and eventually became a national park. How fitting it is that in 2014, forty years later, the blue heron, which had faded from view, is once again a frequent visitor to what is now a precious scenic byway. This quilt celebrates this return.

DEATH VALLEY

"Why should man value himself as more than a small part of the one great unit of creation?" JOHN MUIR

Cheryl Chipman
Program Analyst

In August of 2010, I saw there was a job opening in Death Valley. I had been there numerous times, and thought it would be a good fit. I have been here ever since as a management assistant to the Superintendent. My days are filled with a variety of tasks, from answering requests from the public to planning for the future of the park. Every day brings different rewards and challenges. Death Valley is truly a gem of the universe. Due to its size and differing elevations, the variety of habitats and opportunities is unmatched in any other national park.

I love the light on the mountains as it changes from sunrise to sunset, particularly

Located in eastern California and western Nevada; more than 3,100,000 acres
Established February 11, 1933
Official NPS website: www.nps.gov/deva
- The hottest and driest of the national parks
- Dozens of scenes from *Star Wars* were filmed here

in the Panamint Range. Every day is memorable in Death Valley. Because there are such wide vistas, you can see for miles up and down the valley. I love the roadrunners. They are such unusual beings! It is fun to see them running around with a meal of a lizard or scorpion in their mouths.

Spring is my favorite season here. It is warm, but not too hot, the days are longer, and wildflowers are blooming.

It is not widely known that there is a lot of water here in Death Valley, though it is just below the surface. There are actually several waterfalls in the park. Death Valley is the largest national park in the lower forty-eight states. Ninety-one percent of the park is designated wilderness. We have unparalleled night skies and opportunities for real silence and solitude. Death Valley continues to outlive visitors' expectations with its large landscapes and panoramic views.

Death Valley Days
Carol Younce
Fairfax, Virginia

This scene is a part of my life. I was born in a nearby desert town and often traveled to this area as a child with my family. I love the simple beauty of the desert and the clear and cool nights that bring relief from the heat of the day. My daughter Maren Mecham and her family recently visited Death Valley, and I used her photographs as my inspiration.

Working on this quilt gave me an opportunity to use some special dyed fabric, and I also dyed a piece of faded drapery fabric from my mother's home to use. The differing shades of brown, purple, and blue became the stones and sand of these mountains and this valley. Rebecca Palmer sketched the boots and hand.

Mariposa Lily

Starla Phelps
Alexandria, Virginia

I grew up in Southern California and lived for a time in Yuma, Arizona, so I have spent a great deal of time in the desert. I particularly enjoy spring in the desert. Most people consider the desert to be only sand, but spring can bring a blaze of colors. I decided to incorporate into my quilt the effect of the more than five years of drought and the effect on the flowers. The climate has greatly reduced the appearance of the spring flowers. My husband suggested that I do something in the style of Georgia O'Keeffe, since I have always liked her paintings. Hence, here is the grand mariposa lily.

For the background, I sewed small pastel batik squares together, then on top of that, I wove burlap and two types of raw silk together. Next I fused and sewed them. This represents the harsh, dry, baked sand in which the plants might fight to survive, due to the severe weather conditions. I sewed a few tiny flowers on the background in pale shades of silk ribbon. For the central flower, I cut out three petals of cotton and covered them with silk organza; the center was made using multiple layers of trapunto mesh. The center stamens are crystals. The silk represents the delicacy of these lovely flowers, fighting so hard to survive.

Tarantula

Patricia Dews
Gainesville, Virginia

This piece was a challenge for me. I began research on the Internet, obtaining inspiration from images of Death Valley and tarantulas.

Although I have a large fabric stash, I went on a shopping spree to find just the right special fabric for the desert and the tarantulas. Because the focus needed to be on the fauna, I made a bargello background to reflect majestic purple mountains in the distance, and a large expanse of sandy desert. I felt that would make a good background for the tarantulas. I made the tarantulas by fusing cotton fabric to the background, then satin stitched the edges, and couched yarn all around. Since I wanted to exaggerate the hair on the tarantulas, I settled on a fuzzy yarn.

DENALI

"Nevermore, however weary, should one faint by the way who gains the blessings of one mountain day; whatever his fate, long life, short life, stormy or calm, he is rich forever." JOHN MUIR

Wendy Mahovlic
Visitor Center Front Desk in Winter,
Re-vegetation Technician in Summer

I love Denali and its surroundings. Because I wanted to stay here and use my degree in landscape architecture, the re-vegetation tech job made perfect sense. I have worked here in various capacities since 1992.

Favorite spots abound in this park, depending on the weather. When I look around, the wildness surrounding me calms my soul. Autumn is my favorite season and it is the time when Denali is carpeted with an autumnal palette as far as the eye can see.

In the summer, I ride my bike to work, then a coworker and I drive the park road, where we eradicate invasive plants in June and July. In August, I

Located in interior of Alaska; 6,000,000+ acres
Established February 26, 1917
Official NPS website: www.nps.gov/dena
- Mount McKinley is the highest mountain in North America at 20,320 feet
- This park has a team of canine rangers; these are the only sled dogs helping to protect the wildlife, scenery, and wilderness at a US national park

collect native plant seeds for future re-vegetation projects. In the wintertime, I drive nine miles to work and greet visitors who are lucky enough to visit Denali at that time. I also answer phone calls and e-mails from people who are planning trips to Denali.

Most people don't realize there is much research happening in Denali. One interesting fact is there are 758 native vascular plants in this park, about 1,000 species of native mosses, lichens, and liverworts, and only twenty-nine species of non-native plants. I particularly love the little alpine plants that are so amazingly resilient and hardy, yet at the same time, so delicate and beautiful. Almost every day I witness a landscape or wildlife sighting, or I see a friendly, memorable smile from a visitor or neighbor.

Wild places are important for humans to remember where they came from, to get back to our roots. When we protect them, we protect our origins. These places lift our hearts, calm our spirits, and cleanse our souls.

Denali Inspiration
Priscilla Stultz
Fairfax, Virginia

Two years ago I spent almost three days in Denali National Park. When I heard about this project, I was eager to share my special experience with the world, in fabric.

I was lucky to visit on a day when Mount McKinley was visible. The sun was shining and the sky was beautiful blue with puffy white clouds. As I painted the clouds here, and with each piece of fabric, I could recall standing in awe of the beauty. As I later looked back at my photos, my beaming smile told the story of my enjoyment of the frontier. I was truly blessed to have experienced this in person. May it continue to awe and delight visitors for centuries to come.

This quilt almost made itself. As I pulled fabric to audition, the choices were so easy. The cloud painting happened in moments. The visit to Denali not only affected my thoughts of what beauty is, but it changed my creative nature.

Fireweed
Ann Douglas
Springfield, Virginia

Fireweed is a "pioneer" plant; it is one of the first to recover from a fire or an avalanche. I dedicate this quilt to my nephew, Don. He is a guide who takes people to climb Mount McKinley. After two to three weeks of snow, ice and high winds, Don is thrilled to see the vibrant fireweed in the valley.

This piece was completely made by hand. Kyoko Yamamura helped with the binding and some of the hand stitching; thank you to Jinny Beyer for the "Northern Lights" background fabric.

I like tapping into my personal history to respond to a quilt challenge opportunity. Alaska: the pungent scent of pine trees, views of the Chugach Mountains, frequent sightings of wildlife, northern lights dancing in the night sky, and the taste of wild game and salmon formed my earliest memories. Alaska is my home state, and Denali is my favorite national park. I love experiencing the landscape, terrain, wildlife, plants, and trees of Alaska and of this park.

I especially admire Dall sheep (*Ovis dalli*) traversing steep and often rocky mountainsides of the park. They are tenacious in their footing, and have an ability to find food and to flourish in a harsh environment.

To make this quilt, I enjoyed playing with the images and remembering the fun, awe-inspiring visits to Denali.

DRY TORTUGAS

"How can I close my eyes on so precious a night?" JOHN MUIR

Michael Wydysh
Interpretive Ranger

I chose to work with the NPS because I love the outdoors and I firmly believe in their mission to preserve our natural and cultural resources for this and future generations. I have worked here for about ten months. Dry Tortugas is one of the few places left in the United States where you can really get away from all of the chaos of modern life. With the beautiful waters, spectacular views, and the rich history, one cannot help but be relaxed out here.

I enjoy standing at the top of the fort, looking out at the reefs through the aqua blue water. When I do this at sunset, it is even more spectacular. I also love stargazing at the park. There is so little light pollution, some nights the Milky Way looks like it was painted across the sky. Because of the calm seas and the warm crystal-clear water, summer is perfect for exploring the reefs.

Dry Tortugas is one of the most remote national parks, which makes working here a challenge. The islands can only be accessed by seaplane or boat. It is essential to plan ahead and pack everything you need. If you run out of anything, you have to wait a long time to get supplies, or you have to just make do without. Sometimes even communication with the mainland can be difficult. Once you get past these minor inconveniences, this place is just magical.

The very first underwater black and white photographs were taken at Dry Tortugas in 1908. Then, in 1917, the first color underwater photographs were taken here. I love our coral reefs. The remoteness leads to pristine and undisturbed ecosystems. Every time I get into the water, I see something I have never seen before. The beauty and rich abundance of life never becomes mundane to me. Shortly after the start of the Civil War, Fort Jefferson became a military prison. Some very high-profile prisoners were sent here, including four of the Lincoln conspirators, one of whom died in the Tortugas.

The Dry Tortugas are the "crown jewel" of the Florida Key reefs and of the National Park Service. Whether you are into snorkeling, birding, fishing, or history, you will be taken aback by the beauty of these remote islands.

Located west of Key West, Florida; 64,000+ acres (only 93 acres are above water)
Established October 26, 1992
Official NPS website: www.nps.gov/drto
- This park is only accessible by boat or seaplane
- The unfinished Fort Jefferson is the largest masonry structure in the Western Hemisphere

Old Glory at Fort Jackson

Mary Wilson Kerr
Woodbridge, Virginia

We visited the majestic Fort Jackson in the Dry Tortugas on a crisp but sunny day in early 2010. Everything was beautiful, but I was drawn to the American flag that flew proudly at the top of the brick wall. It gently fluttered in the wind while a million sparkles of sunlight danced all around.

To recreate this scene, I used scraps of vintage lace, old buttons, and an antique flag atop the fragments of a homespun "cutter quilt." Recycled Americana at its finest!

Bay Cedar

Jeanne Coglianese
Fairfax, Virginia

I was not familiar with the Dry Tortugas National Park before I started this project. I chose the bay cedar as my focus after learning it was an original native plant, as opposed to the many non-native and invasive plants that have become so prevalent at the park in the last century. The bay cedar is on the endangered species list for Florida.

Angel Fish

Kerry Faraone
Purcellville, Virginia

I had a huge inspiration for this angel fish. I grew up with the granddaughters of Dr. Samuel Mudd, the doctor who was accused of taking part in the conspiracy to assassinate Lincoln, by setting John Wilkes Booth's broken leg.

He was just one vote shy of the death penalty. He was sentenced to serve his time at Port Jefferson at Dry Tortuga. This was a scant island, devoid of fresh water, where only tortoises (*tortuga*, in Spanish) nested. There was an epidemic of yellow fever in the prison, and Dr. Mudd saved the warden's wife. Because of this, his life sentence was commuted. It took his great-granddaughter, who became a lawyer, to get a full pardon from the US government. Yes, I had a very personal connection to that Caribbean angel fish.

EVERGLADES

Located in southern Florida; 1,508,538 acres
Established May 20, 1934
Official NPS website: www.nps.gov/ever
- Only true tropical forest in the northern hemisphere
- Hosts nearly 15,000 sudents every year on a variety of ranger-guided tours, e–field trips, and special events

"Everything kept in joyful rhythmic motion in the pulses of Nature's big heart." JOHN MUIR

Maria Thomson
Community Engagement Specialist

A visit to the park as a chaperone with my daughter's elementary school "hooked" me to the Everglades. I have worked here for fifteen years now.

The circle of life in the Everglades is as dynamic as it is subtle. It takes a special attitude to discover its magic, but once you do, it will always be in your heart.

The Long Pine Key campground is one of my favorite places in the park. I enjoy camping there, listening to the whisper of the wind between the pines and the singing of the birds and watching the spectacular sunsets.

We have two seasons in the Everglades; the dry season is from November to April and the wet season is from May to October. My favorite months are April and October because there is a kind of calm; small changes allow me to connect to nature.

It is hard to pick one favorite plant or animal from the huge amount of wildlife roaming the Everglades. This was the first national park to be created because of its biological diversity. But believe it or not, one of my favorites is periphyton, a type of algae making life possible by providing food and shelter at the base of the food web. I also love a colorful bird called purple gallinule, and I am still amazed every time I see an alligator bellowing. The

Everglades is the only place on the planet where you can see alligators and crocodiles side by side.

One of the most memorable moments at the park is still happening. We have embarked on a historic restoration. After decades of abuse, people realized that the Everglades was dying. Thanks to public and government support, a restoration program was established. Even though there have been many setbacks as well as political and economic challenges, we are seeing some positive signs proving the efforts are bringing a better future to the Everglades.

The national parks are so very important not only to our country but for the whole world. America's best idea has expanded and many other countries are also protecting their natural areas for future generations. In a time where technology is isolating individuals from nature and face-to-face communication, the parks are providing places for soul-searching and meaningful life experiences.

Everglades Scene
Kathye Gillette
Fairfax, Virginia

Sunlight filtering through the leaves and the combination of natural color with the bright pop of some colorful fungi or flower springing through the undergrowth are fascinating. The moisture trapped under the canopy forces you to push to get through. The undergrowth against the trails and paths humans create is a reminder the forest is primary.

Everglades is primal and has a webwork of raised trails allowing people to walk through. Experiencing the Everglades by canoe is fantastic because gliding through the water, you sense the animal life, just below you, and you see the vegetation growing in from all around. The roots of the mangroves arching down and through each other to reach the water are mesmerizing. It all draws you in and holds you wrapped by its magic.

Ghost Orchid
Su Gardner
Fairfax, Virginia

Outside of my quilting hobby, I enjoy working with my bonsai and orchid collections. I was excited for this opportunity to be able to create a quilt related to orchids. I have spent some time in the Everglades, but was never fortunate enough to see a ghost orchid. This quilt represents what I imagine it would look like if I were to come across one while walking through the park. I used hand-dyed yarn to mimic the roots of the orchid, wrapped around a tree trunk. A single stalk ends in an exaggerated flower, made to look ghost-like through the use of organza fabric.

Nine-Banded Armadillo
Maggie Ward
Warrenton, Virginia

My decision to choose the armadillo came after exploring the vast amount of "armadillo art" on the Internet. These hardy creatures have been represented in so many inventive and creative ways. I couldn't wait to create my own version. Sadly, when I moved on to looking at pictures of actual armadillos, I realized that they are exceptionally homely critters. The only photos that were at all appealing were the ones showcasing mothers and babies. The phrase "a face only a mother could love" seemed fitting.

From there it was a quick decision to make a mother and child. I wanted my armadillos to have an opportunity to dress up and look their very best. These two, mother and daughter, might be headed out to a birthday party or wedding. Or perhaps there are other occasions armadillos celebrate of which we humans are not aware. Many of the laces and trims used in this quilt are vintage hand-me-downs from my mother. Thank you, Mom!

GATES OF THE ARCTIC

"The most extensive, least spoiled, and most unspoilable of the gardens of the continent are the vast tundras of Alaska." JOHN MUIR

Located in northern Alaska; 8,472,506 acres
Established December 1, 1978
Official NPS website: www.nps.gov/gaar
- Northernmost national park
- Contains no roads or trails
- Lies north of the Arctic Circle

Kris Fister
Chief of Interpretation and Education

I believe in the National Park Service mission of preserving and protecting these special places for current visitors. I also want the opportunity to explore and experience them myself! I have been with the NPS for over thirty years, including fifteen years at Denali. I am a very new employee at Gates. This place is the epitome of wilderness, to me. There is spectacular landscape with a climate challenging not only the plants and wildlife, but also the people who have used it first for their livelihood and survival, and now additionally for recreation and escape.

The Brooks Range is calling to me, but I've only been able to see it from the air and from spots along the Dalton Highway. I love the remoteness and vastness of Gates. I am excited about meeting the logistical challenges of getting to the Brooks Range, but I know it will be well worth the effort.

My favorite season is fall. I love the vibrant colors of the tundra vegetation and how beautiful animals look with their new fur coats and antlers, bodies fattened by summer feasting. I enjoy the return of darkness to the night sky, with opportunities to see the northern lights when it's not -40 degrees, and also that the mosquitoes are gone!

Believe it or not, rangers spend a lot of time inside, working in a visitor center or office answering visitor queries either in person or via phone or e-mail. We enjoy helping folks learn more about the park, especially so they can prepare themselves better. Getting to meet visitors from all over the world, even in remote visitor center locations like Bettles and Coldfoot, is one of the best parts of the job. We also do backcountry patrols not only to learn about the park so that we can better pass on information to others, but to perform maintenance or other projects.

Many people don't even know Gates exists, due to its remoteness. Here is a factoid: the name of the Arrigetch Peaks in Gates of the Arctic National Park and Preserve comes from the Nunamiut word for "outstretched fingers." Visits here are not overnight, but are multi-day float trips or overland backpacking treks.

My favorite flora and fauna are the miniaturized plants and the tough animals inhabiting the highest parts of the park, for example, the alpine zone. They all have fascinating adaptations to deal with the harshest environment of an already difficult area to survive in.

National parks preserve ecosystems, habitats, and ranges for endangered species that would otherwise be lost. We inherited this legacy from those who had the foresight to establish the first parks over a century ago, and it is our responsibility to pass it on to future generations. A nation that loses its history, loses its soul. The units of the National Park System were set aside for a variety of reasons. They were not meant to be "one size fits all" in terms of visitor enjoyment or accessibility. Gates of the Arctic, as a wilderness park, will only be experienced in person by a small number of people. But through the Internet, social media, and other means, our virtual visitors can also learn of its significance and hopefully make a connection to this very special place.

Aurora Borealis
Sandy Veatch
Springfield, Virginia

When planning to do a landscape quilt of Gates of the Arctic, I wanted to challenge myself to try a new technique and get out of my usual way of paper-pieced quilting. I used one-inch squares to create a mosaic of an image in my head of the park in late summer when the days are shorter. The northern lights are seen across a dark nighttime sky, rather than being visible above snowy mountaintops. The effect of reflection on the snow and ice makes the lights appear to be everywhere in a spectacular show. But the brilliance in the dark is so much more dramatic, and that is what I wanted to capture.

The visual of the mosaic squares is greater when standing back ten feet or more from this piece. The looming pines on either side of the landscape are what I picture to be the gates, leading into the most northern and remote of the United States national parks.

Arctic Moss
Amalia Parra Morusiewicz
Mitchellville, Maryland

Moss is an important part of the cycle of life in arctic climates. The green line represents the continuous nature of flora. The texture evokes moss covering hidden objects, such as rocks.

This piece was made whole cloth, with fabric, yarn and paint.

Caribou
Shannon Dart
Springfield, Virginia

I love wildlife and Alaska, so I knew right away I wanted to do a fauna quilt. Caribou are a major component of Gates of the Arctic National Park. The painting I did for the central panel was an experiment. I could picture in my mind what I wanted to portray, but I had never painted on fabric before. I am mostly happy with the result. I added a caribou in each of the corners because I enjoy working in wool.

"Give a month at least to this precious reserve. The time will not be taken from the sum of your life. Instead of shortening, it will indefinitely lengthen it and make you truly immortal." JOHN MUIR

Katie Liming
Public Affairs Assistant

I have always been interested in both public service and environmental conservation efforts. Now I have the opportunity to combine both of these interests—and spend my free time hiking and biking in a beautiful place. This is my first summer at Glacier National Park and with the NPS. I had never been to Montana, prior to this summer. In just a short time, I've been amazed by the diversity of flora and fauna I've found. I've also enjoyed biking, hiking, and attending educational programs. I have especially enjoyed meeting other people who are passionate about Glacier. I am excited to be a part of a community that is working to protect such a special place.

In my job, I help communicate the park's mission and news through press releases, interviews, social media, and events. I have the opportunity to work with visitors, community members, and business partners. I enjoy working with our staff to find the clearest way to communicate with visitors and our local community. I love sitting along the shores of Lake McDonald and looking up at snowcapped mountains and down at a rainbow of different colored rocks. It's exciting to see wildflowers popping up all over the park as snow melts away. I love the bear grass and Indian paintbrush flora, and I have a strong affinity for moose.

Glacier National Park and Canada's Waterton Lakes National Park form the world's first international peace park. There are now peace parks all over the world.

We recently celebrated our 100 millionth visitor to Glacier National Park! We all had a great time welcoming that lucky family's arrival. They had the opportunity to take a Red Bus tour up to Logan Pass on the west side on the road's opening day. They enjoyed playing in snow in June and learning about the park's natural history.

Our national parks offer countless economic, cultural, recreational, and health benefits. But our parks are most worth protecting because they provide a critical habitat for plants and animals. It takes an immense amount of time, money, and effort to sustain and protect a park. I am grateful for opportunities to enjoy the outdoors in parks both big and small.

Glacier National Park: Lake Josephine

Nicki Allen
Springfield, Virginia

I have been to the beautiful State of Montana, but not to Glacier National Park. Still, the images I found when preparing to make this art quilt felt very familiar. I quickly discovered inspiration in a photograph by Andy Cook, used with permission. I tried to stay true to his panoramic picture of Lake Josephine, while taking a bit of artistic liberty. I hope I captured the same sense of beauty I saw in his photo. The quilt is machine pieced, machine appliquéd, raw-edge fused, and machine quilted. The water was done in the "tiled" style of Gloria Loughman.

Indian Paintbrush

Jane W. Miller
Dumfries, Virginia

As native Virginians with limited travel experience, my husband and I jumped at the chance to attend our niece's wedding outside Missoula, Montana, in the summer of 2009. Arriving in Spokane, we drove through northern Idaho and western Montana. Aside from the wedding, the highlight of the trip was our visit to Glacier National Park. The snow-capped mountains in late August were only one of the amazing sights. The Going to the Sun Road, the lakes, trails, and waterfalls were each memorable and we enjoyed seeing and photographing them all. Among the memories were so many flowers, a favorite of which was the Indian paintbrush.

Studying a photograph for this project, I was struck by how much the flowers reminded me of Eleanor Burns's and Bonnie Hunter's braid techniques. I decided these techniques would be perfect for the floral effect; the next challenge was finding fabric. A leftover batik from a recent project closely resembled the darker blossoms and a gradated piece in my stash worked as the brighter bloom. I experimented with decorative, variegated threads to replicate the fuzzy edges of the Indian paintbrush. This was a delightful challenge, and it brought back many fond memories of our trip out west.

Harlequin Duck

Marisela Rumberg
Fairfax, Virginia

Because I am from another country, I was always fascinated by the vast array of landscapes in America I would see in movies, on television, and in magazines. Living here for the past few years has given me the opportunity to see in person just how beautiful she truly is. I am very taken by how Americans had the foresight to protect these special places by enshrining them through a system of national parks. When I heard about this project, I jumped at the chance to give thanks for the park system by adding my vision. I am an avid bird watcher and I love to laugh. The notion of the harlequin duck of Glacier seemed a natural choice.

This is a whole cloth quilt. I designed and planned it in paper and then traced only the main outlines of the duck and the mask. First I painted the fabric, and then did some Zentangle designs and black color accents. Everything is free-motion quilted; the background and water were not marked before quilting them. I used my trapunto technique to add dimension.

GLACIER BAY

Located on the Alaska panhandle; 3.3 million acres
Established February 26, 1925
Official NPS website: www.nps.gov/glba
- Largest protected marine sanctuary in the world
- Although most easily accessed by air since no roads lead to it, most visitors see the park from a boat

"Whales and elephants, dancing, humming gnats, and invisibly small mischievous microbes, all are warm with divine radium and must have lots of fun in them." JOHN MUIR

Emma Johnson
Park Ranger, Interpretation and Education

Glacier Bay is special because it remains intact. In other parks, such as Yellowstone, major species such as bison or wolves have been extirpated. Park managers and partners have worked hard to restore the natural habitat. While we continue to monitor for changes at Glacier Bay, there is much less restoration and rehabilitation than in other places. Our habitat and ecosystems are pristine, from the beach meadows to the alpine.

Glacier Bay is full of places of scenic wonder and beauty, but one of my favorite places in the park is the entrance to the Beardslee Islands. These islands are close to the park headquarters, but can only be accessed by kayak at high tide. Though not very far from the developed section of the park, as soon as you paddle through the entrance, it feels like a different world. Harbor seals peer curiously as visitors go by. Loons and murrelets skim across the water. Bear amble along the shores. No matter how often I go there, it always feels new and I always see something that causes me to pause and watch in wonder. Sometimes that is something as simple as the patterns of the kelp in the water. Other times it is the drama of a sea lion eviscerating a fish.

I love that we have seasons at this park. After a long quiet winter, the singing of birds signals that spring is near. Spring flowers in southeast Alaska are understated; I love the small pale pink blueberry flowers and the yellow green tips on cottonwood trees. Summer is exciting and busy, full of visitors to the park. They pick berries, take kayak trips, and enjoy long walks with friends in the light hours, well past bedtime. By the time the birds, humpback whales, and visitors head south in the fall, it is time for the hustle and bustle of summer to wind down. Fall is often extremely wet and rainy, but on the rare clear days, Glacier Bay is stunningly beautiful. Winter is quiet and peaceful, snowy or rainy. I enjoy whatever season we are in, but I appreciate the coming of the next.

Summer is the busiest season. More than ninety percent of the park visitors come by cruise ship and experience the park from the ship. Rangers begin their days early, often by meeting at headquarters at 5 a.m. They gather up their gear and climb aboard the *Serac*, our transfer vessel. The *Serac* meets the cruise ships at the entrance to the bay and rangers climb aboard the cruise ships using a rope ladder. While on board, the rangers set up a traveling visitor center desk, provide commentary from the bridge, present a formal program in the theater, host a children's program, and rove the ship, answering a multitude of questions and talking to visitors. It is a long but fulfilling day.

Many people know that fireweed, those beautiful stalks of purple-magenta flowers, come back after a fire. But what people may not know is fireweed plants are also some of the first things to grow back after a glacier retreats. A plant ecologist, William Skinner Cooper, pioneered the study of plant succession and used Glacier Bay as his laboratory, returning to plots year after year. Glacier Bay was eventually established as a national monument in order to study plant succession and to be used as a living laboratory.

Today, Glacier Bay beautifully showcases the process of plant succession. Next to the glaciers, where they have just retreated from, is bare rock. Lichens come back first, then hardy pioneer plants like fireweed and dryas. Eventually willow and alder take root, fixing nitrogen and adding organic matter to the rock and sand. Cottonwoods are the first big trees to return, followed by spruces and then hemlocks. This entire process can be witnessed while traveling through Glacier Bay!

Margerie Glacier
Karla Vernon
Vienna, Virginia

During a cruise in 2013, I took a wide shot of the glacier called Margerie. Since I planned to do a vertical quilt, I cropped the photo to show just one aspect of the glacier. When enlarged to 20 by 44 inches, the photos's colors dramatically pixilated, giving me a wonderful palette of colors to work with. That is called a happy accident! I used artist's paint sticks to achieve the effect I wanted. The paint sticks proved vital for the details; the addition of crystals and special shiny fibers called "Angelina" gave my glacier some iciness.

My work tends to be more abstract than this quilt. I often work with blocks of color in geometric shapes. I am most inspired by artists who are able to distill complex scenes into simple lines and shapes.

Despite spending the summer in Washington State, I had taken no photos previously of western hemlocks. I looked at many pictures on the web to come up with the design for this quilt, and I tried to capture the "drooping branch" look, which seems to be characteristic of this tree.

Humpback Whale

Ricki Selva
Scott Air Force Base, Illinois

Who can resist falling in love with these gentle giants? The northern waters of the humpback whales' migration are where the whales do all their eating for the year. The humpbacks who winter in the waters off Hawaii and summer in Alaskan coastal waters are some of the best-studied whales on the planet, and yet we still can't translate their body language, when they breach, spyhop, or slap those enormous pectoral fins on the water. I like to think this whale is dancing for joy because his belly is full and he's headed for Maui when the weather turns cold.

GRAND CANYON

"The world, we are told, was made especially for man—a presumption not supported by all the facts." JOHN MUIR

Sharon Ringsven
Deputy Chief of Concessions

I visited a lot of parks in college as part of geology classes, and backpacked in Grand Canyon. As I sat on the Tonto Platform Trail, overlooking the river, I knew I didn't want a job that was predominantly in an office. I always wanted a job that wasn't bound by four walls.

The best part of the day is my walk or bike ride to and from work. The remainder of my day includes the typical technology aspect of work: phone messages and calls, meetings, and e-mails. I also work with our concessioners who provide many visitor needs: lodging, food, and souvenirs.

One of my favorite spots is at Little Nankoweap. Partway up to the Nankoweap granaries are great

Located in northwestern Arizona; 1,217,403 acres
Established February 26, 1919
Official NPS website: www.nps.gov/grca
♥ One of the Seven Natural Wonders of the World
♥ The canyon's native fish are a vital and unique part of the natural ecosystems

views both up and down river where I see the different geological layers of the canyon. I enjoy viewing the granaries, which are archeological sites. My favorite season is the spring. The elevation in the park goes from 2,000 feet down near the river to 9,000 feet at the North Rim, and flowers bloom for months during the springtime.

Many people don't realize Grand Canyon National Park has the only kindergarten through grade 12 school district located within a national park. The first school at the Grand Canyon began in July 1911, one year before Statehood. Today's school serves over 300 students. Also, notable events happen here that change history, such as the 1956 mid-air collision between United Airlines and Trans World Airlines flights over Grand Canyon. This event led to the creation of the Federal Aviation Administration in 1958.

Many of the gems of the National Park Service are the small units, not just the big ones everyone knows. I challenge our visitors to find those smaller units, even as part of a larger vacation.

Hermit's Rest to Watchtower at Desert View
Dorothy B. Dane
Annandale, Virginia

When I began this project, I had just returned from a vacation that included Zion, Bryce Canyon, and both the north and south rims of the Grand Canyon. I interpreted the design for this quilt from my memories of both rims, fresh in my mind. This canyon is over 275 miles long, up to eighteen miles wide, and a mile deep. The Colorado River is large and rapidly moving, but it appears small when seen so far away at the canyon bottom. I depicted a small piece of it in this quilt. Impressed by the architect Mary Elizabeth Jane Colter, I included two of her buildings, seen on either side of my quilt. Hermit's Rest, built in 1914, was designed to look like a miner's cabin. Desert Watchtower, built in 1932, was modeled after the ancestral Puebloan watchtowers. Colter also designed Phantom Ranch at the bottom of the canyon and Hopi House next to El Tovar Hotel. A contemporary of Frank Lloyd Wright, she was a woman ahead of her time and held her own in a man's world.

Pincushion Cactus

Susan Egge Haftel
Gainesville, Virginia

My husband and I enjoy touring the national parks of the West. We are especially enamored with the Red Rocks area, including the Grand Canyon. While exploring, I try to take as many artistic photos as I can and have indeed stumbled into some lovely settings. Unfortunately, this quilt was not a result of one of these photos, and I realize now I may have to invest in a better camera and a macro lens. The photo I used for inspiration I found on www.publicdomainphotos.net.

The cactus flower was translated into cloth through the process outlined in *Repliqué Quilts* by Chris Lynn Kirsch. The flower was made first and was later attached to the finished cactus and rock background. Fine-tuning of color was accomplished with crayons and stamp pad inks, thanks to a consultation with Heather Thomas about the composition of the piece. I used quilting thread tied through buttons to represent the spines that grow through tiny knobs on the plant.

Mule

Ellen Brereton Icochea
Alexandria, Virginia

I have always loved the grandeur of the Grand Canyon. This quilt draws on a memory from early 2006 when I was blessed to enjoy the majestic views while hiking to the bottom of the Grand Canyon, staying a few nights at Phantom Ranch, and hiking back to the rim with my husband George and some close friends. Unfortunately, one of our friends, Steve, significantly twisted his ankle shortly after we entered the park and was unable to walk. A ranger suggested that Steve show up at the Mule Barn in the morning to inquire about cancellations. On the second day, someone cancelled their mule trip and Steve was able to reunite with us at Phantom Ranch. On that day, I learned that the Grand Canyon mules provide multiple functions: they ferry tourists to the bottom, provide food and supplies for the ranch, carry out trash, and take the mail to and from Phantom Ranch. If a guest mails a postcard or letter from the bottom, it is stamped "Mailed by Mule at Phantom Ranch: The Bottom of the Grand Canyon." These sturdy workers truly are icons of life at the Grand Canyon.

GRAND TETON

Located in northwestern Wyoming; 310,000 acres
Established February 26, 1929
Official NPS website: www.nps.gov/grte
♦ The granite and gneiss that make up the core of the Teton Range are some of the oldest rocks in North America, yet these are among the youngest mountains in the world

"The night wind is telling the wonders of the upper mountains, their snow fountains and gardens, forests and groves; even their topography is in its tones." JOHN MUIR

Andrew White
Assistant Public Affairs Officer/Park Spokesperson

My parents always liked to take us kids to national parks for family vacations. Oddly enough, though, I never thought about the parks as a career until I went to college. That is where I became interested in the topic of humans and their relationship to the natural world. I decided to look for an internship with the NPS. I was hired as an interpreter at Grand Teton in 2010, and quickly realized this was the place for me. I've since moved into public affairs, where I work with the media, and tell the park's story to the world.

Grand Teton is the first park I remember visiting with my parents; I was six or seven years old. Years later, my older sister worked for one of the concessioners here and we visited on a number of occasions. The opportunities for adventure at Grand Teton really grabbed me, and they haven't let go. I'm always discovering new spots to love. Whether it's a new alpine lake that I've hiked to, a different section of the Snake River that I've paddled, or a cool ski in the woods, the most recent adventure always seems to trump all the rest. Each season brings its own magic. A lot of people like September because the aspens turn gold, the elk are in rut, and the crisp cool mornings give way to beautiful sunny days. I tend to like June because the snow has melted out of the valley and has been replaced by wildflowers, particularly arrowleaf balsamroot. Hiking trails thaw out in the mountains and provide a renewed sense of discovery.

I personally love great gray owls; they have such a stately presence about them. I also love that people associate them with wisdom, but they really are of below-average intelligence for a bird. It's all a charade! I certainly don't mind seeing all of the wonderful wildlife this park has to offer. It's one of the few places left on Earth where many species, particularly predators, inhabit: grizzly bear, black bear, moose, elk, mule deer, wolves, coyotes, foxes, mountain lions, bighorn sheep, pronghorn, the list goes on and on.

Visitors today often don't realize what a struggle it was to create Grand Teton National Park. There was great local resistance to the idea of creating a park in Jackson Hole. We really owe it to visionaries like Maud Noble, Horace Albright, and John D. Rockefeller Jr., for persisting through this resistance for many decades until this place was finally protected.

The national parks preserve special places for future generations. Parks like Grand Teton are important because they give us a glimpse of what the world would be like if it was left unaltered by humans. Granted, there is a lot of development here, but all of it serves to give people a sense of the natural world. That's something worth protecting.

Landscape of Grand Tetons

Nancy Firestone
Alexandria, Virginia

I saw the Grand Tetons in 1992 on a family trip to several national parks. I was inspired by the beauty of the mountains, as reflected in the lake. I attempted to capture this reflection in my quilt using collage-style artistry. I used many layers of cotton fabrics to "build" the mountains, then added snow, lake, and sky. A dusting of glitter brightened the snow. To enhance the trees in the foreground I added variegated thread and yarns. An overlay of netting over the entire piece allowed me to stitch larger areas of the quilt without having to sew each individual piece of fabric.

Thistle Flower

Trudi Sommerfield
Alexandria, Virginia

In researching flowers in national parks online, I was immediately drawn to the shape, texture, and colors of the thistle flower. In some respects it is more of a weed than a "regular" flower.

I came to quilting fairly late in life, having first tried a number of other crafts. I started out making quilts based on patterns created by others. Soon I became disillusioned with the repetitive process this often requires, and I decided to try my hand at original designs. This suits me better. Many traditional patterns are symmetrical, and I much prefer asymmetry. When making a quilt, fabrics are used much as an artist uses paint, and there are many wonderful fabrics to choose from. I enjoyed selecting fabrics to represent the thistle. Although the plant is basically just pink and green, I used a variety of values and textures of these two colors. I learn much with each piece of fabric art I create. This project was both fun and informative.

Shiras Moose

Betty Tucker Dietz
Ardmore, Pennsylvania

The first time we visited Grand Teton, we brought along our young son. One morning we stopped for a snack break and as I was feeding our son, my husband decided to wander down toward the lake to get better photos of the ducks on the water. Just a few minutes later, he came barreling back up the hill, saying "Moose!!! I saw a moose, and it was close!" He did not get the photo, but I would like to think if he did, it would have looked like the close encounter pictured in my quilt.

This quilt was a real challenge for me. It is the first time I depicted a living creature in fabric. Getting the eyes just right was tricky. I was able to use many of my favorite quilting techniques, like machine appliqué, thread play, and machine quilting. I love the fact that I can choose certain fabrics, and by cutting and stitching them together, I am able to make art imitate nature.

GREAT BASIN

Located in east-central Nevada near the Utah border; 77,000+ acres
Established January 24, 1922
Official NPS website: www.nps.gov/grba
- The park is a desert, with low humidity and lower temperatures at night
- It can snow any time of year at high elevations, and summer is a time for fierce afternoon thunderstorms

"To the sane and free it will hardly seem necessary to cross the continent in search of wild beauty, however easy the way, for they find it in abundance wherever they chance to be." JOHN MUIR

Aileen Carroll
Park Ranger, Interpretation

This park is very remote, and compared to the larger national parks, the number of visitors is relatively low. Even though this is a small, lesser-known park, it is full of hidden gems. From the oldest trees on Earth, to a beautiful, highly decorated cave, to some of the darkest skies in the continental USA, Great Basin has much to offer. The night sky is so dark, if you look straight up you will see the same sky the Native Americans saw 10,000 years ago. You can easily see the Milky Way, and you can even see our nearest galactic neighbor, the Andromeda galaxy, with your naked eye. By the way, in 1963, the sci-fi film *The Wizard of Mars* was filmed here in Lehman Caves. The movie is a spoof on *The Wizard of Oz*!

I especially love the Baker Creek Loop within the park. It is a shorter trail, about three miles, and it runs alongside a creek. You can hear the creek laughing as you walk next to it, and near the top of the loop, you suddenly come out into a huge meadow.

The Great Basin bristlecone pine tree is one of my favorites. This species can live to be over 5,000 years old, and is the oldest living single organism on Earth. These trees are surprisingly small for their age, and are gnarled and twisted. They grow at an altitude above 10,000 feet, and due to the harsh

conditions at that elevation, they grow very slowly. They also have the ability to compartmentalize themselves, and allow some of the tree to die while the living part remains separate. Sometimes you will see a bristlecone that looks completely dead, but when you look closely, you can see a strip of bark that leads to one living branch. This is how the bristlecone is able to survive droughts and harsh winters.

The national parks are important to our country because some things should belong to the American people as a whole: from nationally important historic sites, like Fort Sumter, New Mexico, to natural wonders, like the Grand Canyon, to the diverse wildlife found in parks like Theodore Roosevelt and the Everglades, to ancient cultural landmarks found in places like Mesa Verde. These places are all iconic American landmarks, and should be protected and available for everyone to experience.

Great Basin is quiet and beautiful: a great place to get away from the hustle and bustle so many of us are surrounded by.

View of Mount Wheeler and Stella Lake

Betty Tucker Dietz
Ardmore, Pennsylvania

I'm lucky to have visited Great Basin twice in the past three years. The first time was in mid-summer when my daughter and I were on a cross-country trip along US Route 50. There was not much snow and we were able to hike from the lake to the mountain. I was struck by the contrast between the ruggedness of Mount Wheeler, the smoothness of the ancient bristlecone pines, and the sparkling waters of the lake.

I chose to create my quilt combining the elements of the mountain, the pines, and the lake. By using quilting techniques such as strip piecing and hand and machine quilting, I recreated the scenery. The hard lines of the mountain and glacier are juxtaposed with the smooth lines of the tree and lake. It is inspiring but always a challenge to use fabric and thread in such a way as to capture a scene from nature.

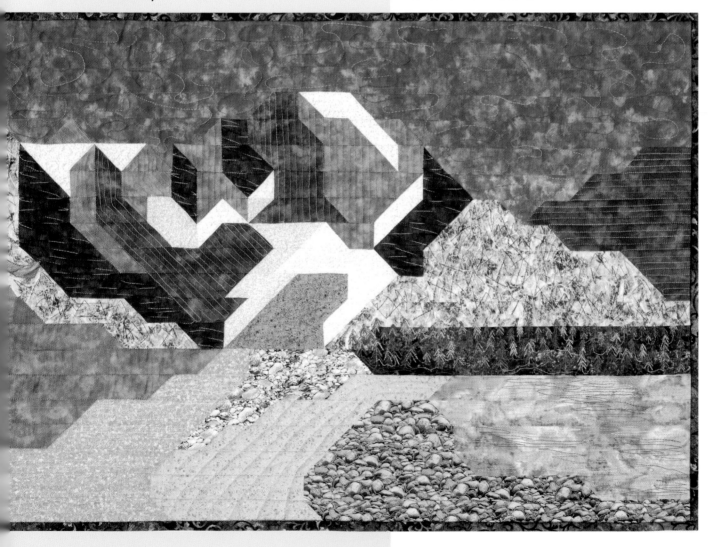

Bristlecone Pine

Polly M. Davis
Warrenton, Virginia

My husband and I have long loved bristlecone pines. These trees are some of the oldest living organisms on Earth and we find this mind-boggling. To me, they are like looking at the face of Mother Teresa: tons of wrinkles that tell a marvelous story.

I tried to convey the age and sheer character of a tree that can live so long in conditions that don't sustain much other life. I layered the twisted fabric and strands of different fibers to show the complexity of this tree. Some areas no longer have bark, since that section is dead. Although much of the tree may be dead, there is still life in some branches. The bristlecone pine lives in rock and scree on mountaintops, battered by wind and harsh conditions. My admiration for this tree is boundless.

Pygmy Rabbit

Meggan Czapiga
Bethesda, Maryland

I was inspired to make this art quilt because of my love for animals, especially rabbits. I was particularly drawn to the pygmy rabbit because there are populations on the endangered species list and I am active in animal conservation. I captured this by shadow quilting many rabbits into the background of my quilt so they are mere shadows; they are barely visible.

I used different tones of brown silk and free-motion quilting to give detail to the burrows these rabbits dig. The pygmy rabbit is one of only two species in North America to dig its own burrow. I made the sagebrush and tall grasses where these rabbits live from fancy yarns and raffia, along with the fabric pattern I chose for the base of the background of my quilt.

GREAT

SAND DUNES

Located in eastern Colorado; 150,000 acres
Established March 17, 1932
Official NPS website: www.nps.gov/grsa
- Contains the tallest sand dune in North America, rising 750 feet
- May is the best time to experience Medano Creek's "surge flow" where waves up to 18 inches high flow across the sand

"Nature's object in making animals and plants might possibly be first of all the happiness of each one of them, not the creation of all for the happiness of one." JOHN MUIR

Matthew Fritch
Administrative Support Assistant

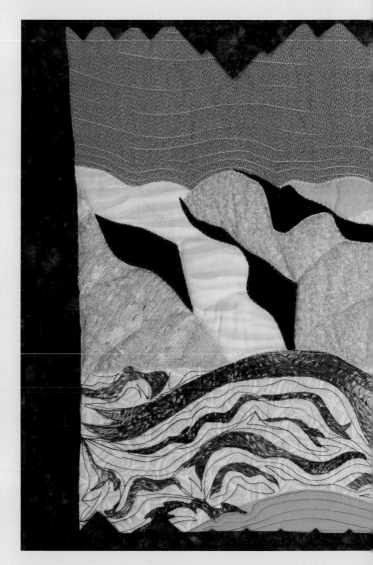

After serving in the military for twelve years and following the three years as a DoD civilian, I believed working at a national park would be a great way to continue my public service. This position, which I have held for the past nineteen months, allows me to serve my fellow Americans in an exciting environment, full of history and natural beauty.

There really is no such thing as a typical day. With my job comes a multitude of duties. I feel I am always doing something different, and I am constantly learning new things. The staff here at Great Sand Dunes is comprised of some of the greatest people I have ever worked with. It is always a pleasure to talk to other staff members and ask them about their jobs. Each and every one of them lights up and goes into such detail talking about the latest interpretive program, the latest findings while out measuring wells, what they saw while readying the campground, or a set of animal tracks they found while out on patrol. It is a great feeling to work with others who so enjoy their job that they can't wait to share the details with you each day.

Medano Pass is my favorite spot, so far. The backcountry area is so beautiful, and it's always full of surprises. Every time I am up there, I see something I haven't seen on a previous trip.

Most people don't realize what a variety of ecosystems we have within the park. "Great Sand Dunes" elicits an image akin to the Sahara, but we have so much more to offer, including alpine tundra.

My favorite flora in the park are the prairie sunflowers. It feels like they sprout up on the dunes suddenly, overnight. The most memorable thing that happened to me to date was coming across a couple of bull elk vying for the alpha position. It was a sight to behold to see these two massive bull elk trying to be the dominant male.

I have traveled the world, but am always amazed at how diverse we are as a nation. I feel the national parks represent this diversity and it is on display for all people of the world to be able to visit and see why America has drawn people to her shores for centuries.

Medano Creek and Great Sand Dunes

Erica Robertson
Fairfax, Virginia

This quilt is based on a photograph I took when visiting Great Sand Dunes with my family in June of 1995. We crossed Medano Creek through about twelve inches of icy cold, numbing, invigorating mountain run-off water, just to reach the dunes. The creek was surging in rhythmic waves on the sand and the sandbars in the creek; this was a local mountain water phenomenon. We then hiked in the sands that swallowed our feet to the ankles or deeper, and we occasionally rolled down the side of a dune for fun. The sun-warmed sands were rippled and contoured by the winds, with vistas stretching to snow-capped mountain peaks reminiscent of the Colorado license plate graphic. In contrast, the sand in the dark dune shadows was noticeably cooler on our feet. These memories shaped the landscape featured in my quilt.

Alpine Forget-Me-Not

Ann Douglas
Springfield, Virginia

I have always loved forget-me-nots. I chose to make this quilt in the spirit of a botanical drawing. The sand fabric on the bottom represents the Great Sand Dunes. The gray blocks going up the left side represent the mountains. The five-petal blossom was so much fun to make with rickrack.

Kyoko Yamamura helped with the binding and machine quilting.

Snowshoe Rabbit

Shannon Gingrich Shirley
Woodbridge, Virginia

I lived in Colorado Springs when I was younger and loved hiking and camping with my family. I always thought of the Great Sand Dunes as a very hot, dry, sandy place. I researched and found out the snowshoe hare was on the list for the park's fauna. Snowshoe hares are named for their large hind feet that act like snowshoes in the winter. The park has an average annual snowfall of thirty-seven inches. The snowshoe hares are almost completely white during the winter. They change to brown during the warmer months, which helps camouflage them in the changing environment.

GREAT

"These blessed mountains are so compactly filled with God's beauty,
no petty personal hope or experience has room to be." JOHN MUIR

SMOKY MOUNTAINS

Located in North Carolina and Tennessee; 521,000+ acres
Established May 22, 1926
Official NPS website: www.nps.gov/grsm
- Elk are being reintroduced to the region, a process that began in 2001
- The wispy smoke-like fog in the Smoky Mountains is from rain and evaporation from trees
- It is the most visited national park

Jamie Sanders
Park Ranger, Protection

I have worked at Great Smoky Mountains since February 2008, including seven years as a law enforcement ranger. My father and I made several weekend excursions a year to the Smokies, beginning when I was eight years old. It was on one of those trips, at age eleven, that I decided to become a ranger at the Smokies.

I still remember the October day during a hike up to Mount LeConte via the Alum Cave Bluff Trail. While my dad and I were at the bluff enjoying our lunch, a family came down the trail from above and warned us there was a mother bear and cub approximately a quarter of a mile up the trail. My dad and I, being fairly new and inexperienced to the great outdoors, quickly ended our lunch so we could try to catch a glimpse of the bear ahead. When we reached the location, the cub was the only bear visible. The cub was in a tree, off the trail and up a very steep and densely vegetated embankment. After determining we were at a safe distance, I dropped my pack so I could grab my camera. We could hear mother bear walking through the dense vegetation above, but we could not see her. I quickly reached for my camera to snatch a few photos of the cub, and at about the time I got ready to go "click," mama let us know she was not happy we were there. She stood on her hind legs, clearly visible to my dad and I, and growled a bone-chilling growl. She then quickly charged down the hillside, heading straight for us. My dad quickly yanked me up, tucked me under his arm, and took off running, my feet dangling behind him. We were afraid for our lives. When we turned the corner in the trail, my dad looked back to see where mama bear was, and she was nowhere in sight. It was clear to us that mama bear had bluff-charged in an attempt to make us move on. Point taken! This was my first exposure to adrenaline, and I was hooked!

Before this particular trip to the Smokies, I was forced to make a tortuous decision for an eleven-year-girl: whether to go hiking in the Smokies with my dad or to go to a Halloween slumber party with all of my girlfriends. I chose hiking with my dad, and was I ever glad I did. When we returned home, I went back to school and told all of my friends I got charged by a bear during my trip to the Smokies. I was the talk of the school for the day, and it was a weekend I will never forget.

My dad and I continued our weekend excursions to the Smokies well into my college years. Over those years of hiking together, I learned hiking is therapeutic to the soul. As a young teenager, I lost my best friend to leukemia, and I brought that pain to these mountains. At age fourteen, I changed schools and had to make all new friends. I brought all of those challenges to these mountains. My first experiences with love, heartache, notable setbacks, and numerous difficult life decisions—I brought all of it to these mountains. This is where I find solace, strength, wisdom, clarity, insight, and empowerment. Once I got to the age when it was time for me to leave the Southeast and begin my life journey, it was comforting to know that no matter where life took me, I would always have Mother Nature and the national parks there to help me.

October in the Smoky Mountains is our busy period for park visitors, and the bears are active. The fall color is incredible. I get to be a part of those awe-filled moments daily, moments when a visitor gets to see a bear in the wild for the first time. It is rewarding to see that look in a child's eyes and to see just how much that moment is impacting his or her life. I am fond of the hemlock trees. When I was a child, I remember taking note of a hemlock tree while on a hike with my dad.

When we got back home, I looked it up so I would know the name of the tree: eastern hemlock. To see the devastating effect the wooly adelgid has had on the hemlocks saddens me deeply. Treatment methods are working, and park biologists are doing everything they can to ensure the eastern hemlock does not suffer the same fate of the American chestnut.

A typical workday is very busy, and no two days are ever quite the same. During the busy season, from May through October, there is never a dull moment. We see it all, from search and rescue operations, to vehicle accidents, arrests, bear jams, and emergency medical situations. Some days are emotionally difficult but other days are extremely rewarding and full of excitement.

One especially memorable period was the 2013 government shutdown, when the park was closed for two weeks. I saw the wildness return to the wildlife in Cades Cove. The Smokies is so loved that a large percentage of our wildlife have become accustomed to being surrounded by people. After those twelve days of total solitude, I drove around the Cades Cove Loop Road in preparation for our re-opening and saw the wildlife react to my return. More than twenty deer ran at full speed when they saw my patrol vehicle.

The national parks are our forefathers' greatest idea! Thank you to the men and women who fought and who still fight so hard to preserve and protect our Nation's greatest treasures.

Echoes from Cades Cove

Mary Ellen Hardin Simmons
Johnson City, Tennessee

The Smoky Mountains were described by the Cherokee Indians as *shaconage* for the soft, blue, smoky haze that often covers the ridges and descends to the valleys and hollows. In my quilt, I tried to visually capture the feeling of the blue haze and mist over the mountains. This quilt represents my impressions of this park and my trips to the park in past years. This past summer, I explored the park with my granddaughter, Marlee Jean Jennings. We toured Cades Cove, climbed Clingman's Dome, and drove to Oconaluftee and on to Cherokee, visiting many sites and taking pictures. On another weekend, I visited the Cataloochee region of the park. My daughter Liane, son-in-law Mark, granddaughter Chelsea, and I hiked, picnicked, and climbed the steep hills to the cemeteries where we took more pictures. On the trips to the park we saw much wildlife, including deer, box

turtles, and elk, and we even caught a brief glimpse of a black bear as he scurried away and disappeared into the woodland. During these trips, I experienced the beautiful, peaceful and enveloping beauty of the Smoky Mountains.

I make quilts to record and translate ideas and feelings into tangible objects. The play of light and shadow on the hills near my home, people waiting at a bus stop, children splashing in the surf, old barns, and the soft glow of candlelight are a few examples of the things that inspire me to create. Making quilts is my way of depicting memories and scenes of daily life, allowing me to leave a record in cloth and thread. In this work, I have sought to chronicle my impression of vast natural beauty of the Great Smoky Mountains as well as the rich cultural heritage left behind by the early settlers who lived, worked, hunted, farmed, and worshiped in the area.

Galax Flowers

Diane E. Herbort
Arlington, Virginia

Wildflowers often have evocative folk names, accumulated over time. The galax is also known as beetleweed, wand flower, or wand plant. One of my challenges in making this quilt was to make an interesting asymmetrical composition within a square format. Placing the plant off-center, with its flower "wands" waving, gave me the start I needed. During college I worked in a florist shop. We received shipments of shiny green galax leaves to use as the base for nosegay-style wedding bouquets. How different it is to come across a galax growing on the edge of woodlands. Galax plants are now a threatened species, harvested to the edge of endangerment. Poachers often rip up plants, roots and all, so they cannot propagate.

In the autumn, the leaves turn shades of red and bronze. I exercised my "artistic license" and toned down my hand-painted leaves so the summer-blooming plant could remain the star. After trying several arrangements of the leaves, most looked too neat and orderly. I preferred a more random placement. Outlining each leaf and flower required many stops and starts and changes of thread color, but this was just what the quilt needed.

Synchronous Fireflies
Laura Robertson
Kearneysville, West Virginia

For two weeks each summer, during the firefly mating season, the night skies at the Great Smoky Mountains glow with the glittering and magical effect of millions of courting fireflies. These spectacular light flashes are a courtship ritual used for mate selection. Each species flashes light in a particular pattern. In some species, the male fireflies flash in unison, creating beautiful synchronous bursts of light that alternate with periods of darkness. This quilt is designed on two levels: approaching the quilt from afar, the viewer witnesses the bright, dramatic yellow flashes of light. As the viewer nears the quilt, the detail of a flying male firefly can be seen flashing his light for the female firefly as she rests on a blade of grass.

This quilt was made using commercial cotton material and raw-edge techniques.

Located in west Texas; 86,000+ acres
Established October 15, 1966
Official NPS website: www.nps.gov/gumo
- Due to the hot, dry desert conditions throughout much of the park, most animals there are nocturnal
- Best wildlife viewing occurs near permanent water sources

"And as we go on and on, studying this old, old life in the light of the life beating warmly about us, we enrich and lengthen our own." JOHN MUIR

Michael Haynie
Park Ranger

In celebration of graduating from college, I went to Big Bend to camp, hike, and backpack. My degree was in a liberal arts field, and I knew I would need an advanced degree to be employable. I also realized I would most likely face a career that was stressful and not necessarily well-paying. When I was outside I was happy, and the Big Bend trip provided lots of time to do some soul-searching. By the end of it, I had decided to go back to school in a natural science field and seek employment with the NPS. Four years later, my dream came true and I got my first seasonal job at Guadalupe Mountains National Park. That was sixteen years ago, and I've been here ever since.

Guadalupe is remote, rugged, and biologically diverse. Most of it is wilderness, so it offers outstanding opportunities for solitude. Because you have to travel by foot or horseback to most places, you're more likely to notice and appreciate the little things. It's a great place to rekindle wonder.

I love visiting the forest found in The Bowl. It consists of conifers: Douglas fir, ponderosa pine, and southwestern white pine. It's like a little bit of the Rocky Mountains surrounded by the Chihuahuan desert. The hike on the way up, and the high points near the forest, offer views that extend over 100 miles, and the trail winds eventually to a meadow that feels like a hidden realm, since you have to hike down from the ridge at the edge of the forest. Everything about it is different than the surrounding terrain. It's cooler, the air smells like pines, and the sounds of mountain chickadees and white-breasted nuthatches gently rise and fall out of the silence.

There's a lot more desk and office time than you'd think in this job. I frequently staff the visitor center, welcoming and orienting visitors to the park. I am also involved with desktop publishing, so there is quite a bit of time spent on the computer. My favorite shifts are when I am able to spend time outside. I keep a bird and flower list so I'm able to share that information with visitors, lead occasional guided hikes for school groups, and sometimes just make a quick trip down the nature trail near our visitor center to chat with newcomers.

This park is unknown by most Americans, but it is well-known by international geologists. Containing more than 500 types of fossils, and an exposed fossil reef with associated lagoon and ocean basin deposits, Guadalupe is a premier paleontology park.

We have had flash floods, fires, and winds over 100 mph. To see the power of nature is an awesome experience; these are also reminders of how quickly things can change. I have had experiences with wildlife that may seem more mundane, but were memorable and important to me. One day I heard a flock of bushtits making very distressful sounds. They were hopping and flying around the end of a juniper branch.

I approached slowly and discovered that one of their flock was trapped in a large orb weaver spider web. I watched with fascination, but before I even really had to wrestle with the moral dilemma of interfering and saving the bird or letting nature take its course, it was able to get out. Once it did, the whole flock flew away and left me feeling like I had seen something rare.

Guadalupe Mountains National Park is a gem. Many discover us on their way to Carlsbad Caverns National Park, and if they're willing to walk a little, they are pleasantly surprised by the beauty and natural quiet they find here. Crossing miles of desert to discover the story of an ancient sea and reef is amazing, and knowing that there is a bit of the West that remains wild gives people a sense of hope. There are lots of ways to value this place.

El Capitán Memories
Janet R. Palfey
Fairfax, Virginia

I visited Guadalupe Mountains in early 1982 while I was stationed at Fort Bliss, Texas. In this quilt, I wanted to capture the range of blueness in the sky and the rugged, stark beauty of the high desert mountains that had at one time been part of an ancient ocean, then a food source for Native Americans, then a stagecoach stop, and now public parkland. For the land portions of this piece, I chose the most dramatic colors from the range of what I might see at all times of the day, and in all types of cloud cover.

Maple
Diane Graf Henry
Springfield, Virginia

A popular tree at Big Bend is the *Acer grandidentatum,* or bigtooth maple. I dedicate my quilt to the people and families whose properties contributed to all of the wonderful parks in the national park system. I appreciate the gift of beauty and peace these parks have brought to my life.

This scorpion is phosphorescent; he glows in the dark. I used a reverse appliqué technique with raw silk to capture this effect.

HALEAKALĀ

Located on the island of Maui in Hawaii; 30,100+ acres
Established August 1, 1916; detached from Hawaii National Park in 1960
Official NPS website: www.nps.gov/hale
🛡 Local legend says the demigod Maui imprisoned the sun here in order to lengthen the day

"Beauty beyond thought everywhere, beneath, above, made and being made forever." JOHN MUIR

Honeygirl Duman
Acting Supervisory Park Ranger

Almost five years ago I was hired as part of the Student Career Experience Program in interpretation and education as a park ranger. In 2013 I became a lead ranger and in 2014 I was made the acting supervisory park ranger in interpretation. During a visit to this park, my mother-in-law suggested I work here. Thanks, Mom!

I was born and raised in Maui. But not until learning my grandmother's native tongue, Hawaiian, and taking a Hawaiian ethno-botany class, did I truly appreciate its splendor. Once I learned about all of the rich cultural and natural resources, I needed to teach other people these things.

I don't have a favorite spot in the park because all aspects and elevations of Haleakalā are unique and offer different resources, views, and experiences. From the coastal district to the alpine windy and sometimes sleeting environment, I am intrigued by it all. Summertime is a favorite season because the air is filled with the sweet honey fragrance of the 'ahinahina (silversword) and the buzzing of the bees pollinating them.

This park is home to many endangered species of forest birds, many of them endemic, found nowhere else on Earth. The kiwikiu (Maui parrotbill) is endemic to Maui, particularly to Haleakalā. There are only approximately 500 of

these birds remaining in the wild. There is also something very special about the pueo (Hawaiian short-eared owl). As you drive within the park boundary, don't be surprised if the pueo looks at you while it flies during the day across the landscape. All other birds are quiet as the pueo approaches.

Not a day passes by that I don't see work here as a blessing. As a park ranger, I am able to give back to my people and my 'aina (land). My day can start at 4:45 a.m., and soon after I teach people about the resources found only at Haleakalā National Park. I watch peoples' faces brighten up as they learn while making a connection to their own lives. This is my reward. I love this place and my job.

These parks are not just aesthetically pleasing, but are brimming with resources important to the health and success of our society. They offer resources rich in culture, nature, history, seashores, recreation areas, battle sites, and so much more. People from all over the world come to the United States to partake of the resources we are protecting and managing for generations to come.

Mount Haleakalā
Cheryl Stanczyk
West Patterson Air Force Base, Ohio

My landscape evokes memories of our family visits to the beautiful island of Maui and to the lookout area at the top of the mountain. Hawaii is the land of enchantment; rainbows are beautiful to see from the top of the volcano, as is the barren volcanic soil with varying colors. This is the place where I felt like I was walking on clouds at the top of the mountain as the volcano peeked out above the clouds. The bicycles show one of the many visitor experiences available: riding down from the visitor area to the bottom on lava roads in over four hours. This region transitions from desolate and barren mountaintops to lush green foliage-covered forest, then to the ocean crashing against the rugged lava coast. The volcano is home to one of the most important atmospheric observatories in the United States. Once you experience the beauty of the islands of Hawaii you will always long to return. Haleakalā National Park is a site not to be missed.

Sandalwood

Eileen Doughty
Vienna, Virginia

There are many species of sandalwood around the Pacific. Because of its lovely fragrance, many cultures used the wood or its oil, particularly in religious rituals, for incense, medicines, architecture, and carvings. Hawaiians named their sandalwood the iliahi.

When I researched the flora of Haleakalā, I was attracted to this tree because of the beautiful complementary colors of its red blossoms and large green leaves. Further investigation dismayed me, specifically the economic and ecological havoc the iliahi trade caused Hawaii, beginning around 1790.

Within twenty years it was their major export. Hawaiians were displaced from agriculture and fishing in order to provide labor for harvesting the wood. When it became scarce, they would set fire in the forests to locate stands of the remaining trees, detecting it by its sweet smell as it burned. By 1830, the iliahi had all but disappeared from forests, and the Hawaiian economy collapsed. Today, the iliahi grows high on Maui's less-accessible volcanic slopes, particularly on Haleakalā.

My quilt shows various aspects of the iliahi, including the wood grain, and dimensional leaves with the fruit shown in the quilting. A lonely surviving tree is imagined with the Haleakalā volcano looming in the distance. Honoring traditional Hawaiian quilting, I developed a design of the leaves and blossoms; are those volcanic craters or stumps?

I grew up on 'I'iwi Street in Honolulu, a word pronounceable only to locals (pronounced ee-EE-vee). I remember going to the Bishop Museum and seeing red, yellow, and black feather capes and headdresses worn by Hawaiian royalty and being amazed by the delicacy of the feathers. The 'I'iwi bird was one of the sources for the red feathers. I was delighted to make a quilt celebrating this image, evocative of my childhood and Hawaii's heritage.

I am interested in transformation: changing fabric and paper by dyeing, discharging color, painting and embellishing the surfaces, cutting apart and putting the pieces together in different ways. Seeing the transformation is magical. It was serendipitous to already have the background fabric for this quilt, which I had made as a discharge and shibori dyeing sample. It looked to me like an abstract representation of volcanic rock and forest plants that are part of the 'I'iwi's habitat.

HAWAIʻI VOLCANOES

"Fresh beauty opens one's eyes wherever it is really seen, but the very abundance and completeness of the common beauty that besets our steps prevents it being absorbed and appreciated. It is a good thing, therefore, to make short excursions now and then to the bottom of the sea among dulse and coral, or up among the clouds on mountain-tops, or in balloons, or even to creep like worms into dark holes and caverns underground, not only to learn something of what is going on in those out-of-the-way places, but to see better what the sun sees on our return to common everyday beauty." JOHN MUIR

Jay Robinson
Park Ranger

I have worked at Hawaiʻi Volcanoes National Park for twenty-three years, first in the role of the supervisor of the rangers and volunteers. For the last twelve years, I've worked to plan, research, and design exhibits (museum and roadside exhibits, park brochures, and nature trail guides) for park visitors.

My family is from North Carolina and we spent a lot of time outdoors together, exploring streams, caves, and forests when we visited my grandparents in the mountains. I studied biology in college and worked summers at a large Boy Scout camp, teaching kids so they could earn nature merit badges. On the weekends, I spent a great deal of time hiking and backpacking in the national parks and forests of the southern Appalachians. It seemed natural to apply for a summer job as a park ranger between my junior and senior year of college. I scored a great job at the Great Smoky Mountains National Park and wow, it was a terrific summer. It was a lot of hard work, but it was one of the most incredible places on Earth. I helped people plan their trips in the visitor centers, led long nature hikes, and presented slide programs in the campgrounds during the

Located on the island of Hawaii in the state of Hawaii; 323,000+ acres
Established August 1, 1916 (split into Haleakalā and Hawaii National Parks in 1960; redesignated Hawaiʻi Volcanoes National Park in 1961)
Official NPS website: www.nps.gov/havo
The endangered sea turtle comes to shore to nest here. Only one in 5,000 hatchlings survives to adulthood.

evenings. When I graduated, I could think of absolutely nothing greater I could do in life than to continue a career as a national park ranger. For nine years I moved between summer and winter seasonal jobs in different parts of North America; jobs that took me to Cape Hatteras National Seashore, Joshua Tree, Everglades, Denali, Katmai, and Gates of the Arctic. I landed my first permanent position in law enforcement and resource management at Cape Lookout National Seashore. It has been thirty-five years now, and I have loved working in the national parks from the very start.

I love being outside in nature and Hawai'i Volcanoes is diverse and amazing. This is a place where you can hike for days along the rugged coastline, which is mostly cliffs and sea arches, but with beautiful little beaches here and there. There are also opportunities to stroll through tropical rainforests, backpack in the desert, or climb to the summit of snowy Mauna Loa, all in one park.

The plants and animals here are like no place else on Earth. Very few species found their way here, but those that did evolved into some of the most extraordinary forms of life on the planet. It seems like every new plant, bird, or bug you find has an adaptation story that will blow your mind. The Hawaiian culture is alive, thriving, open to sharing, and totally encompassing. Their love of music, language, dance, and closeness to the natural world are infectious.

Did I mention we have erupting volcanoes? Since I first arrived, we have had eruptions. Although we can hike right up to the lava flow, there are also giant lakes of lava where it is best to keep a distance from. The eruptions never get boring because they are always changing and doing crazy new things we weren't expecting. Hawaiians call the lava "Pele" (goddess of the volcanoes) and I have never seen anything so mesmerizing or beautiful. Yet at the same time lava and eruptions are scary. The raw power is on display and is more than a little humbling.

My favorite spot in the park is always changing; it is right at the front edge of a lava flow at sunset. The heat is enormous, the crackling sounds are hypnotizing, the smell is slightly suffocating, but to sit and watch rocks being born is like nothing else imaginable. As the sky grows darker, the red glow of the living rock holds your imagination and fills your being.

We have weird "seasons" here, the wet (in the winter) and the dry. I enjoy hiking and exploring the park without rain (in the summer), but at the same time, I know it is a blessing. Without the rain, we wouldn't have the forests and all they have to offer. But it is a little cooler in the winter and that's when it can snow on the mountains. I've always liked playing in the snow!

My workdays are varied, depending on which project I am involved with, or what the volcanoes decide to do. One day I find myself in the field learning from volcanologists, botanists, birders, or the insect people. The next day I spend time learning from our kupuna (Hawaiian elders) about the history or spiritual side of a topic. I train other rangers and park guides, which involves much time and planning. Every month or two, I stop everything and update exhibits about a new or changing eruption and how people can view it safely.

One of the active volcanoes at Hawai'i Volcanoes National Park is Mauna Loa. It is ginormous! From the sea floor, to sea level, to its summit, Mauna Loa rises nearly 32,000 feet tall! And it is massive. Over 10,000 square miles of rocks comprise that one mountain. Mauna Loa is bigger than the entire Sierra Nevada mountain range in California and Nevada; it is the biggest mountain in the world.

I have so many favorite plants and animals. I find, photograph, and learn about cool plants and animals. Some of my favorites are rare and close to extinction. To learn more about what our national park rangers are doing to save some these beauties, check out a brochure I wrote about them (On the Brink of Extinction, Paradise in Peril) at www.nps.gov/havo/learn/nature/onthebrink.htm. Click on each plant or animal and discover a fascinating story of struggle and survival.

Since I do photography for the park, sometimes I get to fly in a helicopter to remote eruption sites. We always stay in the air, out of the way of the geologists working on the ground, and at a safe distance. A couple of years ago I was on a flight with the park superintendent, when the geologists radioed the pilot and asked to use our helicopter for a little while. The boss agreed and soon we landed and found ourselves within a few hundred yards of a new crack that was opening up and spewing lava hundreds of feet into the sky. I put on safety gear and was able to approach the eruption to take photos. I kept back from where great glows of molten globs were falling, but gosh, what power! The heat was so intense, I had to keep turning from one side to the other, to cool down. The sound was similar to standing next to a giant sputtering jet engine. The whole time, the ground was vibrating and shaking. It was a great afternoon! If you would like to see a video another ranger took of that eruption, see www.nps.gov/media/video/view.htm?id=FCFB7BD7-E0BD-A2E8-B5F030AD9C6B83FD. (Look for me standing near the spattering fountain about two minutes into the video.)

National parks are a uniquely American idea to preserve and protect our combined heritage to enjoy now and for future generations. The most amazing of our country's natural wonders and breathtaking landscapes are preserved in these exalted parks. Without this protection, you or I might not have the chance to see and experience them for ourselves. Without further protection by us and by our children, the future generations may never have these opportunities. Visit as many national park sites as you can, and as often as you are able. If you cannot get to all of the parks, visit them on our National Park websites. Nothing is better than living life through firsthand experiences, but a virtual visit isn't a bad second place.

Do Not Wear Sandals When Hiking on Lava on a Volcano Trail

Elly Dyson
Annandale, Virginia

I went to Hawai'i Volcanoes in 1968 with my family. My husband was born and raised on the island of Oahu and had been to the volcano when he was young. At that time, my son John was four and my daughter Karen was seven. We went on day and night trips to tour the island of Hawaii to see the effects of Kilauea, which was erupting that year.

We walked four miles on Halema'uma'u trail across the volcano. My daughter and I discovered it isn't a good idea to hike in sandals on lava. It rubs your feet like a pumice stone. The floor of the Kilauea walk was mainly gray and black pahoehoe, a smooth lava, that I imagined a moonscape might look like. There were many steam vents and a little vegetation in the lava. We saw spectacular fireworks from the volcano at night and went on many excursions around the Big Island by day to see black sand beaches. These were formed when the lava hit the sea and exploded. This has eroded over the years, and lush greenery appeared, due to the fertile soil and temperate climate.

'Ama'uma'u Fern

Ann Weaver
Roanoke, Virginia

This fern is so graceful and elegant. I was initially intimidated about how to do justice to its beauty in fabric. Randomly, I came across some gorgeous gold cord in my basement. It was divine intervention. I began looking for the perfect background fabric that would make the cord stand out, and found a swatch of upholstery fabric that has the graceful, fern swirl woven into it. The fern swatch was just large enough for three panels on this quilt, to which I attached the cord with a zig-zag stitch. The blue-green batik and blue Hawaiian print fabric seemed to be perfect additions to complete my quilt.

Ginny Rippe helped with artistic design and the use of color, and Martha Rhodes helped with artistic design in placement of the orange fabric.

King Kamehameha Butterfly

Kay Lettau
Annandale, Virginia

My first trip to Hawai'i Volcanoes Park was to accompany my husband on a site visit in conjunction with his position at the National Science Foundation. This visit gave me a sense of what it must be like on the moon. It was inspiring to see life of flora and fauna in such extreme conditions. As we reached the research station, I had my first sensation of altitude sickness. Later visits were much more comfortable as I was properly dressed and knew what to expect. I now have family living in the beautiful state of Hawaii.

Although I began this quilt with traditional Hawaiian appliqué by hand, the additional techniques I decided to use went beyond what I usually create. I enjoyed the process of making this piece and I appreciate the help I received from my fellow quilters.

Thanks to Su Gardner for the machine quilting she did in the background.

Located in central Arkansas; 5,400+ acres
Established April 20, 1832 (proclaimed Hot Springs Reservation; redesignated 1921)
Official NPS website: www.nps.gov/hosp
▼ Includes portions of downtown Hot Springs, making it one of the most easily visited national parks

"Warm, mellow summer. The glowing sunbeams make every nerve tingle." JOHN MUIR

Nalissala Allen
Park Guide

This park is located in my father's hometown. It is where he was born and raised. I spent many summers here with my grandparents, collecting the thermal water and taking it home to drink. Now both of my grandparents have passed away, but the tradition of collecting the thermal water continues with my family. I have always had a great connection to the outdoors and to this park. I have worked here for about five years.

There is no place in the park "in nature" where you can hop into the thermal water. Our water is 143°F, and it is said to be approximately 4,400 years old. To experience it, you must use one of the two operating bathhouses.

Because it is in the city, there are mainly small animals in the park: squirrels, chipmunks, raccoons, possums, deer, fox, and rabbits. There are two life forms that live in the thermal water: the Trelease's blue green algae and the ostracod.

I enjoy all of Hot Springs National Park, but my favorite place is the Stonebridge area. It is the only wetland area in the park.

As for some interesting facts, Hot Springs, Arkansas, was the premier baseball spring training site from the 1880s to the 1940s. The Chicago White Stockings, Cincinnati Reds, Pittsburgh Pirates, Boston Red Sox, and others came to soothe their

aching muscles at the many bathhouses using Hot Springs National Park water. In May 1862, Arkansas Governor Henry Massie Rector moved the state government to his hotel and bathhouse located on Hot Springs Reservation, now Hot Springs National Park. That July, the government seat was moved further south to Old Washington for the remainder of the Civil War. Hot Springs National Park ranger James Cary was the first NPS ranger to be killed in the line of duty. He was shot by bootleggers while patrolling West Mountain on March 12, 1927.

Hot Springs is both the oldest national park, and the smallest. We are the only park federally mandated to give away the natural resource we protect.

America's national parks and historical sites embody the American spirit. They help us remember who we were, who we are, and who we will be. They are windows to our past, homes to some of our rarest plants and animal species, and places where every American can go to find inspiration, peace, and open space.

Hot Springs: My Hometown
Wendy McQuown,
Fairfax Station, Virginia

Hot Springs National Park, Arkansas, is a beautiful city in Central Arkansas surrounded by spectacular lakes and forests. It also happens to be my hometown. Because there are actual hot springs running under the whole area, the Native Americans, who were the first settlers in the area, used what were thought to be medicinal properties of the water in the place they called the "Valley of Vapors." It was a non-warring territory where everyone could enjoy the waters in peace. It is impossible to see the springs running underground, but you can go to one of the bathhouses along the street shown in my quilt, or go to an area with public faucets, and fill up containers with steaming water. Incidentally, the big building is the Arlington Hotel. It is where my wedding reception was held. It is a great place to stay if you visit this wonderful park.

Thanks to Elaine Stemetzki, who machine quilted the background of this quilt.

Tulip

Susanne Miller Jones
Potomac Falls, Virginia

Tulips in full bloom create a riot of color and velvety texture. Constructing a tulip couldn't be done with printed cottons or batiks; I tried. The piece screamed back at me, "make me shiny!"

So out came the charmeuse, satin, crepe, and lining fabric. Even the thread wanted to be shiny, hence the "Razzle Dazzle" and holographic thread.

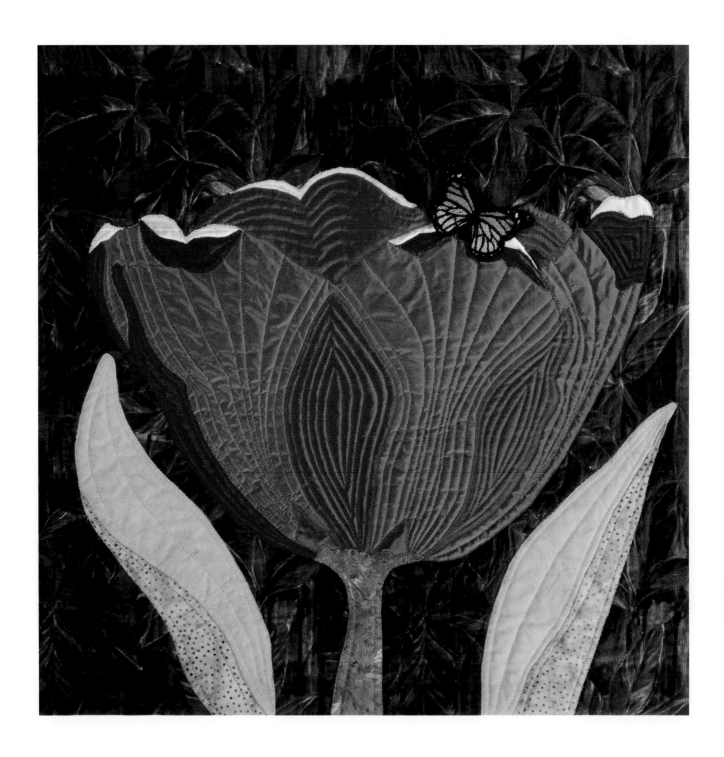

Green Treefrog

Susan M. Bynum
Falls Church, Virginia

I chose to depict the green treefrog for my National Park quilt because I have always been fascinated by tree frogs and their amazing colors. I used all scraps from my scrap basket to make this quilt. I drew my frog on a piece of muslin fabric and then began gluing the fabric scraps (with fabric glue) piece by piece until the drawing was covered. I cut out the frog, making the leg and feet separately. Once the pieces were where I wanted them, I quilted the tree fabric first and then added the frog by machine appliqué. I quilted the frog by sewing around each glued piece. I learned this technique from reading Susan Carlson's book *Serendipity Quilts*. I have made several quilts with this technique and I love the outcomes. I will warn you, though, it gives you yet another reason to keep even smaller and smaller scraps!

"Pure sunshine all day! How beautiful a rock is made by leaf shadows! Those of the live oak are particularly clear and distinct, and beyond all art in grace and delicacy, now still as if painted on stone, now gliding softly as if afraid of noise, now dancing, waltzing in swift, merry swirls, or jumping on and off sunny rocks in quick dashes like wave embroidery on seashore cliffs." JOHN MUIR

Kate Keller
Park Guide

I will begin my fifth season at Isle Royale this summer. I first worked here in 2010 as a Student Conservation Association (SCA) intern, in 2011 as a volunteer-in-park, and since then as a ranger. I have worked as a park guide in the interpretation division the entire time.

How did I did I decide to work for the NPS? Chance. And the fact that it chose me. I went to school and studied urban and regional planning. During my senior year of college, I had no prospects after graduation, so I decided to apply for an internship through the SCA. I applied for what seemed like hundreds of them. Out of that huge pile, only one called me back: Royale. With lots of customer service experience, they thought I maybe had what it takes to live out on the Island for three months and give interpretive programs to visitors. They were right.

This park is special to me for many reasons. First and foremost, it is the place that I reconnected with nature again as an adult, so I'll always be in debt to the Island. A close number two is that I saw the love of my life the first moment I stepped off the passenger ferry at the dock at Isle Royale. I have also since discovered a passion for inter-

Located north of the Upper Peninsula of Michigan, in Lake Superior; 571,790 acres
Established March 3, 1931
Official NPS website: www.nps.gov/isro
♦ Ryan Island, on Isle Royale's Siskiwit lake, is the largest island on the largest lake on the largest island on the largest freshwater lake in the world

pretation and connecting people to places and stories through the work I do. I have found what I love to do.

When I think about places in the park, I absolutely love Windigo. It is where I've had the pleasure to live and work for four summer seasons. Considered the banana belt of Isle Royale, it's always a little bit warmer than most other spots. It is nestled in Washington Harbor, which is gorgeous and calm. Lake Superior proper is intimidating and awesome, but I prefer the protected feel of Windigo.

Every season at Isle Royale is special and unique in its own way, but I'd have to say my favorite month is June. June is peak wildflower season on the Island. Where I'm from in central Illinois, wildflowers are not commonplace; corn and soybeans are! My first summer on Isle Royale I felt as if I were in an enchanted forest that I'd only seen in a movie or read about in a book.

I would describe a typical day in one word: awesome. I walk to work on one of the park's trails, enjoy the sunrise, and then open up the visitor center. Throughout the day visitors stop by with questions about a particular flower they saw or to describe a moose encounter. When ferries arrive with visitors we greet them by giving Leave No Trace orientations and filling out backcountry permits. Then, I might give a guided interpretive hike on the park's trails and an interpretive talk about the cultural history of the Island. I often become a photographer, capturing memories for groups in front of the National Park Service Windigo sign. Perhaps a call will come in on my radio about an emergency involving a visitor, so I'll relay messages to protection rangers and help out where I can. After a very busy day of answering questions, greeting ferries, and doing anything else that needs to be done, I close up the visitor center and take the quaint trail back home.

My favorite statistic to share with visitors is this: Isle Royale is the least visited national park in the lower forty-eight, but has the highest visitor retention rate of any national park. More people come back to this island wilderness than to any other park. I think this is because of the profound effect being here has on people. There is no other place quite like it.

I love thimbleberries. In August there are blood-red thimbleberries everywhere for as far as the eye can see, and I am able to spend hours eating these sour delights. I also love to make jam out of them. It is a novelty in the Upper Peninsula of Michigan and in northern Minnesota.

Our world is rapidly changing and has been doing so for quite some time. Wild places need to be preserved not only for our own sake, but for the flora and fauna that make up the ecosystems. As we continue to develop and grow, our world is becoming more and more fragmented. Trying to preserve it is essential now, but also for future generations to discover, grow, and learn from.

Isle Royale National Park is the best-kept secret in the Midwest. I'm from Illinois, where there is nothing "cool" except for Chicago. They're all wrong! Head north, to the last bit of true wilderness east of the Mississippi. You'll be glad you did.

My husband and I spent our first anniversary on this island, implanted in Lake Superior. We planned our meals, campsites, and hikes. But we did not plan for squalls, the unexpected driving force of the wind, and white-capped waves. As we faced the torrent of waves, we desperately plunged our canoe paddles deeper into the water. Rounding a rocky tip of land, we safely coasted into a cove.

Years later, I am excited to honor Isle Royale. For this landscape quilt, I chose to depict a glimpse in time, the

early 1800s, when the Ojibwe tribe connected with this land. This is where the Ojibwe people mined copper for beads and simple tools. The women made beaded bandolier bags and the men wore celebratory porcupine hair roaches with eagle feathers. If you look closely at my quilt, you will see copper embedded in the rocks with representational oxidation on the shoreline. I hope you catch the gaze toward the Ojibwe symbol in the sky and perhaps hear the whisper of the Ojibwe word *minong*: "a good place."

Lichen

Nancy Karst
Springfield, Virginia

Who can resist the love story of fungus and algae finding each other and discovering they are better together than apart? Though their relationship is chemically complex, when the partnership is right, the two live symbiotically ever after. The results of their union are lichens for us to admire.

Lichens are nature's embellishments on walls, wood, stone, and foliage. We can find them up, down, and all around us in the outdoors. The variety of color, shape, and texture of lichens begs our attention. We all need more symbiosis in our lives.

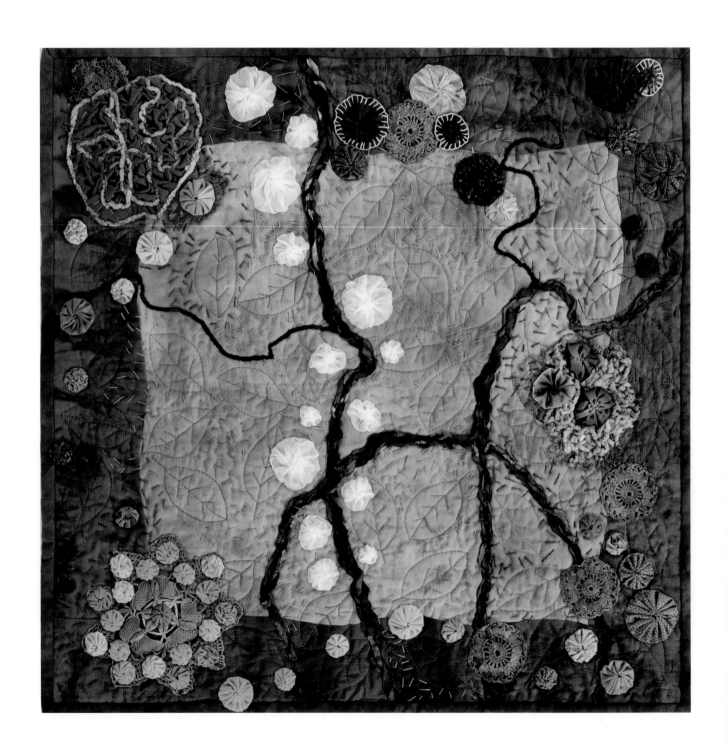

Wood Duck

Lisa Arthaud
Warrenton, Virginia

There are words to describe absolute faith, and then there are actions. While watching a video clip of baby wood ducks, willingly leaping from their tree nests, I was mesmerized by their instinctual trust in hearing their mother's call.

These ducklings are hatched up in tree cavities as high as fifty feet off the ground. They are born with feathers, but have wee wings, compared to their body size. I wanted to hold out my hands to catch each one, comical and fragile.

"Looking at our continent as scenery when it was all wild, lying between beautiful seas, the starry sky above it, the starry rocks beneath it, to compare its sides, the East and the West, would be like comparing the sides of a rainbow." JOHN MUIR

David Denslow
Lead, Visitor Center Operations

I have always wanted to be a park ranger. I have been in this area since 1988. My twenty-year career in the military was in administration, and my college degrees are in business administration. When the secretary for the Superintendent position opened, I was able to fulfill my lifelong dream. I have worked at Joshua Tree since May 2002.

This park is so peaceful, graceful, and unique there are hardly words to describe it. It is amazing to walk among the giant boulders and move among the beautiful Joshua trees; there is solitude and serenity here. There are many hidden gems in this park, and when I walk around the historic sites, I often feel the presence of the miners, homesteaders, and Native Americans who walked these lands in years before me. My favorite spot in the park is the Desert Keys Ranch. For nine years now, every time I present a tour or even visit the ranch, I seem to feel the presence of the Keys family, their children and grandchildren, and the many other visitors who have walked these grounds in days passed. Tours have been conducted here since 1972, so there has been many a footprint before mine. A trip to Joshua Tree is not complete without visiting the Desert Queen Ranch and learning the story of

Located in southeastern California; 789,000+ acres
Established August 10, 1936
Official NPS website: www.nps.gov/jotr
- The tallest Joshua tree in the park is forty feet tall and about 300 years old
- One of the best spectacles in springtime is the blossoming Joshua trees

how the Keyses were able to survive the harshness of living in the desert. This location is not open to the general public, and can only be seen by reservation. Joshua Tree remains open during the winter. Our normal season runs from October to May. The summer months bring many international visitors. I love the entire year at this park because of the diversity of visitors; every day brings something new. I often find myself at a point where I can hardly wait to get to work. March and April brings "Spring Break USA," when wildflowers bloom, and it is an extremely busy time. As many as 300,000 visitors come during these two months alone. In 2005 we had 265,000 just in March, because of the tremendous wildflower bloom that particular year. Visitors come from all walks of life, and people from every nationality around the globe visit us on a regular basis. It is the interaction with these folks that makes every day most enjoyable for me.

One of the most interesting things about Joshua Tree is the many splendid boulder formations and the different shapes of these boulders. Their uniqueness has been weathered by time for many centuries; these majestic granite formations have survived the toughest of storms, yet they are gentle giants. These boulders bring climbers from across the globe to test their skills and to master the challenge of the climb.

For those who want to visit and explore the night skies, Joshua Tree offers some of the darkest in North America. This is the place to come to see the beautiful Milky Way span the horizon like a splendid rainbow.

My favorite flora here would have to be the icon of the Mojave Desert, the Joshua tree. This species is found in only four states. Each tree has its own individual spirit and its own special look and features; no two are the same.

Joshua Tree National Park has inspired many people. From painters to musicians, from poets to authors, this park has seen many artists. They include The Eagles, America, Mama Cass, Eric Burton, Bill Walton, Robert Plant, James Cagney, and Lou Diamond Phillips. This is a park to come to for inspiration and to get those creative juices flowing.

The national parks are important to the United States and are well worthy of protecting. They were each created for an individual reason. They represent something unique and interesting to the millions of travelers who venture from around the world. I have heard often from our European visitors how much they wish their homeland had national parks. The parks are something created and not made; they represent specific times throughout history that will never occur again. They are significant examples of nature or historic buildings that symbolize important eras. Our children deserve to be able to visit these many landmarks dotted across the country and to experience our bounty of splendor.

Keys Ranch

Beth Shafer
Fairfax, Virginia

As a college student taking an astronomy class at California State University, Fullerton, I was encouraged to experience the heavens without city lights. One of the best places to view a clear sky was at Joshua Tree National Park. In the daytime, there were old ranches, rocks, and deserts to explore. At nighttime, the light show began. The naked eye was treated to meteor showers, planets, and so many stars that it boggled the mind. Telescopes expanded the view even farther. From this park, the universe could be seen in all its glory.

Many years later my daughter Meghan would make the same trip and see the same ranch and the same stars. Admittedly, there is more rust and fewer Joshua trees than when I first experienced it, but it is mostly unchanged, thirty years later. My daughter was smarter than her mother. She came equipped with a camera. Her pictures and my fond memories inspired this quilt.

Desert Poppy

Norma T. Fredrickson
Berryville, Virginia

Our family lived in Twentynine Palms, California, located at the edge of Joshua Tree, for eight years. I came to appreciate desert landscape; it was strong in shape and texture, my favorite aspects of visual art. Usually color was a symphony of earthy neutrals paired with paint box sunrises and sunsets. During our desert years, there was the bloom of a century. Sandy terrain became a floral carpet. The same year, I saw a sailboat on a temporary lake. On an afternoon expedition with a desert gardener, I beheld a bright poppy floating above the desert floor on a mere thread of a stem; audacity and delicacy danced in the breeze.

I chose to depict that poppy in this quilt, including the suggestion of a snake in the sand and the shadow of a bird of prey's wing. To live in the desert is to live in a sculpture garden, and to know you are not the owner.

Dark-Eyed Junco
Tom Anderson
Fairfax, Virginia

The dark-eyed junco is one of the winter migrant species of Joshua Tree, and it remains there into March.

Thanks to my wife Judy Anderson for her help on the binding, sleeve, and label of this quilt, which I made with cotton prints and batiks, using a raw-edge appliqué technique.

KATMAI

Located in southern Alaska; 4,093,000 acres
Established September 24, 1918
Official NPS website: www.nps.gov/katm
🛡 There are many active volcanoes located in this park

"All who have time should go prepared to camp awhile on the riverbank, to rest and learn something about the plants and animals and the mighty flood roaring past." JOHN MUIR

Diane Chung
Superintendent, Katmai National Park and Preserve, Aniakchak National Monument and Preserve, Alagnak Wild River

I am here because I love national parks and doing conservation work on public land. I've been Superintendent for two and a half years. Katmai offers vast wilderness, abundant wildlife, volcanoes, and incredible scenery; I love it all. Days when I get out of the office are filled with awesome experiences in different areas of the park accessed by plane or boat. I get to spend many weekends at Brooks Camp, talking with staff, visitors, checking on projects, and viewing bears. I most like fall: no bugs, lots of bears wandering around, fewer tourists, and cool, crisp weather.

We have a long-term partnership with Explore.org that provides live streaming webcams at several areas around Brooks Camp. This allows millions of people to "visit" Katmai who would otherwise not be able to get here. Brown bears are my favorite, especially cubs. They are totally adorable, but they have a tough few years ahead for them and their mothers, just trying to survive.

The population of the world keeps growing. It is critical that we save wild places where nature dominates and natural processes are allowed to go on with minimal human impacts.

Kassandra Grimm
Brooks Camp Interpreter

I started training in King Salmon in May 2015 and arrived in Brooks Camp May 12. I work as an interpreter, staffing the visitor center, presenting programs and managing bear and human interactions. I decided to work for the National Park Service because I find the mission inspiring, and it allows me to live and work in beautiful places.

Katmai is special: I find the opportunity to witness numerous bears so close very special and unique. Brown bears are the major attraction for visitors to Katmai National Park. They each are individuals who exhibit perseverance to survive in this environment. Katmai is a wonderful wilderness park with lots of bodies of water for recreation. My favorite spot is Fures Cabin in the Bay of Islands.

A typical day includes bears in camp, bear jams due to bridge closures as a result of bear activity, and bears on Naknek Lake Beach in front of camp. During the month of July, bears can be seen at Brooks Falls catching salmon migrating to spawn. As an interpreter, we present many bear orientations a day in the visitor center, open and close the bridge based upon bear activity, and ask visitors to wait or move to different locations to minimize bear/human interactions. While managing the bridge and crowds of people, we interpret the bears' behaviors to visitors.

Katmai National Park was created to preserve the area impacted by the 1912 eruption of Novarupta for the purpose of studying volcanology. The Valley of Ten Thousand Smokes was not the result of the eruption of Katmai as was believed for several decades. The eruption of Novarupta was the largest volcanic eruption of the twentieth century, and no human lives were lost.

National parks are important; a great portion of this country was wilderness when it was founded, creating a key aspect of the American spirit.

Brooks River
Lisa Chin
Salt Lake City, Utah

The Brooks River area of Katmai is the most visited portion of the park, due to its abundance of fishing and brown bear sightings. I was attracted to this part of the park because of its beautiful river and mountains in the distance. I took inspiration from the colors and varied texture, recreating a scene using free-form piecing and hand-dyed fabrics.

Purple Marshlocks

Paula Golden
Blacksburg, Virginia

Potentilla palustre (purple marshlock) grows in bogs, marshes, wet meadows, creek banks. and lake margins. It is used as a tea in native Alaskan communities. Red dye is obtained from its flowers, and the root is an astringent. It is said to have been used in the treatment of dysentery and stomach cramps.

The connectedness to times past and present is an important variable in my choice and use of materials. Using fiber as a creative means to communicate is intrinsic to my very being. It links me to the continuum of men and women who have stitched their lives in fiber to provide warmth and nourishment for the body and soul.

Brown Bear and Salmon
Karen Mudry Avil
Great Falls, Virginia

Because the brown bear was the mascot of my son's school, I made several quilts with the brown bear theme. This is the first time I tried to use snippets in fused appliqué. The new technique allowed me to compose the subject with texture and shading. These salmon are on the start of their trip upstream to spawn. The brown bear positions itself in the river to catch migrating salmon.

KENAI FJORDS

Located in south-central Alaska; 670,000 acres
Established December 1, 1978
Official NPS website: www.nps.gov/kefj
- The park contains the Harding Icefield, one of the largest in the US
- Ice in the glaciers of the fjords flows downhill at about twenty inches per day

"Here you glide into a narrow channel hemmed in with mountains that are forested down to the water's edge. There is no distant view, and the attention is held to the objects close about." JOHN MUIR

Kristy Sholly
Chief of Interpretation

I have worked at Kenai Fjords since the spring of 2006. I decided to work for the NPS when I discovered there were still places in the world where a person could get lost. This job is my way of being able to share my love for special places, and it is a means to help others connect to ensure their stewardship for the future. Kenai Fjords is a dynamic place where mountains, ice, and ocean meet. I never thought I would fall in love with being in Alaska, but I connect with this place and the local community.

My day begins by putting on my park ranger uniform and preparing to connect visitors to the dynamic landscape within the park. On any given day, a ranger staffs a visitor center, presents a program at the Alaska Sea Life Center, narrates a six-hour boat tour to the fjords, or guides a hike to the edge of an ice field.

I love the feeling of being in a kayak in view of a massive tidewater glacier. When the ocean is calm, you can hear the thundering sounds of movement within the glacier, the popping of air escaping from icebergs, and the sounds of seals moving through the water. I love to feel the cold that blows off a massive ice field. In those moments, I feel very connected to this landscape.

I love the spring. After many months of darkness and snow, color comes back to the landscape. The rainforest turns lush and green, the whales return, and the birds are singing again. More than half of this park is covered by ice. The interconnections between mountains, ice, and ocean create a rich ecosystem where many animals can thrive. Puffins are amazing. They are one of the most colorful and charismatic birds of the fjords. Not many birds can fly better underwater than in the air! After they have eaten too much, it is fun to watch them try to fly. They can barely make it off the surface of the water. It is always exciting when the puffins return from their time out in the open ocean in the springtime to nest.

Something memorable happens in our park every day. This is one of the few places on Earth where you can witness geologic processes in a human time frame.

The national parks are important because they are a reflection of who we are as Americans, and of what we value. They help to tell the story of this nation's natural and cultural heritage. Kenai Fjords is one of the undiscovered gems of Alaska. It is a special place where a visitor can stand on the edge of a vast ice field and hear the sounds of thousands of nesting seabirds and glaciers calving into the sea.

Kenai Fjord and Glaciers
Bonnie Anderson
Haymarket, Virginia

For this project, I returned to my love of mosaics and created a landscape representation of the Kenai Fjords. I experimented with a technique from a workshop I took by Cheryl Lynch at the Mid-Appalachian Quilters annual educational seminar. This quilt is not of a specific view but it is a collage of many of the natural features we saw while visiting this park: mountains, fjords, avalanches, ice fields, fireweed, and several types of glaciers (alpine, tidewater, calving, cirque, and hanging).

When looking at the finished piece, I find myself forgetting the minutia and details of the time-consuming step-by-step procedures. I step away from being the artist and see it from the onlooker viewpoint: appreciating the piece as a whole.

Salmonberry
Dianne Harris Thomas
Fairfax, Virginia

My husband was stationed at Fort Richardson in Alaska for his military service, and we took our children to Alaska many years ago, so this state is very special to me. We got to see Denali on a crystal-clear day, along with grizzly bears and Dall sheep, a moose ambling across the road as we watched slack-jawed from our car, soaring eagles off the Kenai peninsula, salmon running in a brook, and a beluga whale in the Turnagain Arm.

Most of the composition of this salmonberry plant was done as a colored-pencil drawing. I depicted the startling fuchsia flowers and the glistening red and orange berries on this quilt. I have many art quilts in my head, visions waiting to be made real. This is exciting work.

Puffin

Karen R. Wolfson
Chantilly, Virginia

I am a quilting voyeur. My artistic process begins with insinuating myself into a supremely talented group of quilters. This is usually through my talented quilting mother (Nancy Adams) and my willingness to sous sew (like sous chef, but with fabric) for her quilting friends. Once accepted into the guild, I wheedle my way into their fun challenges, like this one.

My current subject matter comes from a child addiction (until recently in remission) to puffins.

Two species of puffins nest in Kenai Fjords. Puffins are awesome. Puffins are what you get if you pay for the upgrade on a penguin. The "clown of the sea" is a fitting focus for a sewing sidekick.

I wanted to tackle this challenge from a playful angle. I made a fiddly-precise border, but a puffin decided to step out into it. Careful hand appliqué was paired with what-the-heck attempts at fused appliqué and free-motion quilting. Yoyos? Sure! Ultrasuede? Why not? But the solid black fabric is actually the reverse side of a black and white print, because even I couldn't countenance paisley puffins. After all, a henchman needs to show some restraint.

KOBUK VALLEY

Located in northwestern Alaska; 1,750,716 acres
Established December 1, 1978
Official NPS website: www.nps.gov/kova
- One of the least visited national parks
- The western Arctic caribou herd migrates to and from their calving grounds through the park
- Arctic wilderness survival skills and gear are needed to visit

"Yonder rises another white skyland." JOHN MUIR

Linda Jeschke
Chief of Interpretation

My love of nature, from spending a lot of time working on the family farm, and a love of education, from experience in nature centers and environmental education camps, is what caused me to work for the National Park Service. I have been here for fifteen years. This park is special to me because with no roads, trails, or typical visitor services it is challenging to get to. This park provides a remarkable wild experience for those who choose to visit. America has fewer and fewer wild places where park visitors can enjoy the challenge of being self-reliant. This place provides an opportunity where people are able to discover the park for themselves.

The eastern edge of the great Kobuk sand dunes shows a fascinating transition between sand and forest. Carpets of lichen are beautiful, and the (mostly) firm footing for hiking is a real treat, compared to the squishy tundra surrounding the area. Late August is my favorite time at the park; the berries are ripe, and the fall colors are magnificent all across the tundra. Mosquitoes are also a little less abundant.

About 235,000 caribou migrate across the park twice a year. This leaves trails in the tundra and across the mountains that look like deep grooves across the landscape. The historic Giddings Cabin at Onion Portage is a National Historic Landmark. The great Kobuk sand dunes are now about twenty-five square miles, but the dunes used to be closer to 300. There is no new sand being added and plants are colonizing the edges of the dunes. The Kobuk locoweed, *Oxytropis kobukensis*, grows nowhere else in the world. It can only be found on the sandy dunes in the southern part of the park.

In 2013, a fiber artist named Elaine Phillips created a gorgeous tapestry as part of our Artist-in-Residence program. It traveled around the state as part of the *Voice of the Wilderness* exhibit. It shows the Onion Portage cabin and many of the natural features nearby.

Kobuk Valley protects a unique feature of the landscape, which is subsistence living. People have harvested plants and animals here for thousands of years, and current laws enable them to do that today as well. This park protects the health of the things that people harvest (fish, caribou, moose, green plants, berries) so the story of people living on the land can continue.

At Midnight on the Fourth of July in Kobuk Valley

Elly Dyson
Annandale, Virginia

I learned about Kobuk Valley from information on the Internet. Because Kobuk is entirely north of the Arctic Circle, the sun does not set there on the Fourth of July. I learned about the caribou, the orange rocks on the Kobuk River bank, and the three sand dunes. I found out there are no roads or designated trails in the park.

I am intrigued by descriptions others write about a subject. I try to figure out how to interpret words into a meaningful design.

Locoweed

Carol C. Eberhardt
Orchard Park, New York

I learned so much about Alaska and about quilting techniques while creating this quilt. Imagine this little plant, the Kobuk locoweed, enduring the harsh conditions in the Arctic Circle, with extremes in temperatures and weather conditions. It was very challenging to find images and to work with so few available to make a likeness. I learned how to use watercolor, and I also learned not to do that again. I learned that fusible batting is my new best quilting friend. I finally like raw-edge appliqué, and I learned that the process is as important as the product.

As a quilter, what motivates me first is fabric: the colors, textures, lights and darks, how they play together. From there, I think about what will showcase those beautiful colors and textures best. In this case, I began with a theme. My first thought was, where are all of those fabrics I bought in Alaska in 2009? I was inspired by the simplicity of this flower, and initially, by its name. "Loco" at first led me down the crazy patch path, but that didn't showcase the flower well. I decided to focus solely upon the flower, and to build a background to draw the eye to it.

Singing Vole

Joyce L. Carrier
Purcellville, Virginia

I like to use all types of fabrics and threads in my projects, and there are no restrictions when I create. In this piece, I layered fabrics on the top, which is a hand-dyed rayon. I then cut away layers to reveal a lower layer, and I embroidered on top of this. I worked in pebbling, meandering, garnet stitches, and bobbin work, allowing me to use heavier cording than would normally fit through a needle.

When I found a little creature at Kobuk Valley National Park actually called a singing vole it immediately caught my attention and made me smile. The singing vole derives its name from its chirping sounds, which may be territorial noises or warnings of danger. Inspired by the idea of a vole actually singing, I created a little fellow standing in the grasses, wearing a tux, and singing with his heart to an audience we can't see.

A favorite quote, "I think I'm painting a picture of two women but it may turn out to be a landscape," by Willem de Kooning, is a constant reminder that art evolves. You may not end up with what you first designed!

The grasses were inspired by istockphoto/dimonspace, and some of the flowers were inspired by Shutterstock/Helga Pataki.

LAKE CLARK

Located in southwestern Alaska; 4,030,015 acres
Established December 1, 1978
Official NPS website: www.nps.gov/lacl
- Can only be reached by boat or small aircraft
- Lake Clark is 1,056 feet deep and covers 128 square miles
- The area is dominated by two active volcanoes

"Wander here a whole summer, if you can. Thousands of God's wild blessings will search you and soak you as if you were a sponge and the big days will go by uncounted." JOHN MUIR

Megan Richotte
Chief of Interpretation

I decided to work for the National Park Service because I don't know anywhere else where I can live and work in some of the nation's most spectacular and special places, or where I would get to spend my time helping the public come to know and understand their public natural and cultural heritage. I have worked here for five years.

The Cook Inlet coastline of the park is a wild and remote area with some of the richest habitat in the world for coastal brown bears. Saltmarshes, salmon runs, and clam beds support some of the world's densest bear populations, and this is why it's my favorite area of the park. The time of year I like best is the month of June. The weather is often spectacular. Following nine long months of a brown and white color palette, June introduces a world turning green with splashes of wildflowers.

Lake Clark is often called "Little Alaska." Its four million acres hold craggy mountains, active volcanoes, boreal forest, tundra, shimmering turquoise lakes, wild coastline, and spectacular wildlife. A lifetime could be spent exploring just this one park.

Volcano, Cabin, Glacier, Salmon Stream

Nancy B. Adams
Annandale, Virginia

Living in Alaska for more than four years was an awesome experience for me, an untraveled city girl at the time. Everything was superlative: the tallest, the coldest, the most serene. Going berry picking for lowbush cranberries and having to watch out for bear, moose stopping by our back yard to munch on the shrubbery in the winter, going for a hike late on a summer night while the sun was still out: every day had a new surprise or challenge. It was easy to notice the "big" things at first: the mountains and the weather extremes. I learned to see and appreciate the tiny wildflowers and berries that cling to the ground where they can stay warm enough to survive, scraggly trees growing in permafrost, animals enduring the cold and making the most of the short summers.

I loved doing the landscape for Lake Clark National Park because it contains a bit of everything that makes Alaska so wonderful. There are tall mountains and glaciers, active volcanoes spewing steam and ash, gorgeous lakes with blue water, salmon streams, and historic cabins that were built before the area became a national park. There is also the wonder of all the wildlife inhabiting this beautiful place so close to the city of Anchorage. One small landscape couldn't hold it all, so I cheated and did five scenes instead.

Black Spruce

Dolores Marcinkowski
Fairfax, Virginia

I lived with my husband and children in Alaska for over three years; this was his first "overseas" assignment in the Army. We loved living in Alaska. The children went to school at Fort Richardson. Many times they were late getting home because of the moose on the school steps; they had to wait until the moose left the area before they could leave school. We were always happy for long summer days. We took many pictures of the beautiful scenery and visited several parks. We hoped to visit Lake Clark, which could only be reached by air. Unfortunately, those plans were cancelled when the Great Earthquake happened on Good Friday in 1964. We left Alaska just a few months after that.

I have seen many pictures of Lake Clark and am sorry we missed seeing it in person. I imagined the many beautiful evergreens and the huge pinecones, and this was the inspiration for my quilt.

Bald Eagle

Jennifer Weilbach
Littleton, Colorado

The original sketch for this eagle was drawn by my son, Dustin, for a stained glass piece chosen by his high school senior class for the artwork in the school's grand entrance. For this quilt, I placed the eagle into an Alaskan setting, as if landing on a cliff face. The ruffled feathers represent the harsh conditions of Alaskan weather.

A collection of national parks quilts wouldn't be complete without a bald eagle. Our bird from the last state of the union is attacking the unseen predator on the cliff, perhaps near a nest of newly hatched eaglets.

My quilts are about the fabrics I choose, and how they interact with each other. Feathers are not solids; neither are batiks. The shadings and undulations, the light and dark, the wind and weather show the speed and tension of the approaching wild and ferocious animal. I quilt to evoke emotion in others, sometimes cozy comfort, sometimes shock and awe. I use fabric, pattern, design, and color to create a story with pictures instead of words, to surround people with love and beauty as well as a sense of their purpose and existence in the world.

Located in northeastern California; 106,000+ acres
Established May 6, 1907
Official NPS website: www.nps.gov/lavo

- All four types of volcanoes on Earth are represented here
- The area was a meeting point for the American Indian groups Atsugewi, Yana, Yahi, and Maidu
- The reddish color seen at times on top of snow here is snow algae, a living organism being studied for cancer-fighting properties

"All the rocks, as if wild with life, throb and quiver and glow in the glorious sunburst, rejoicing." JOHN MUIR

Shanda Ochs
Park Guide, Interpretation and Education

I have worked at Lassen since 2000 year-round, so a day is not "typical." Winter varies greatly from summer. Since I work with visitors, my day usually depends on how busy visitor centers are. A summer day might look like this; prepare for the day with important pertinent information to relay to visitors, manage desk duty with ranger programs and breaks. I am the lead at one of the park's two visitor centers. Then I make sure information and bookstore items are well stocked, and I keep communications open with other park staff regarding Visitor Services.

I have several favorite places within the park, but I don't want to give them away! I feel people can find their own special places that have meaning for them. I love late summer through early fall, when the temperatures cool, but days are still long, and the shadows get a little longer. Some of the wildlife are very active, looking for food to store for winter.

This park is physically situated in a confluence of three separate biologically diverse ecosystems, with influences of each interacting with the other, making the park quite biologically diverse. I love trees, in particular, conifer trees. There are twelve different conifer tree species that reside throughout the park. Different regions, based mostly on elevation, determine what species of tree grows there. However, one particular spot has eleven of the twelve species in a small area. Those are along the Lily Pond Nature Trail.

Greg Marcinkowski
Biological Science Technician, Wildlife

The national parks have been an important part of my life for as long as I can remember. Growing up in the suburbs of Washington, DC, the mountains of Shenandoah were my escape to a more wild, scenic place. I never got tired of the endless trails through the rolling Blue Ridge, finding swimming holes during muggy summer days, or the amazing display of color during the fall. In fact, I don't think I even visited another national park until I was in college, unless you count the National Mall. I had seen the pictures of Delicate Arch and Half Dome and yearned to experience those sites for myself.

When I first made my way across the country, I was amazed at the grandeur of the West. The endless vistas, big mountains, and stunning rock formations were hard to conceive. I was so excited to start hitting some of the national parks I had seen in the postcards, and upon arriving, they were much more than I had expected. What can prepare you for some of those sites? Certainly not postcards or pictures on Facebook.

What I remember most about those first parks I visited are not the main attractions that everyone wants to see, but the feelings I got once I stepped onto the trail. Away from the noise and crowds, I felt like I truly experienced the parks and developed a connection I've never let go of.

There is so much our national parks have to offer, and I had barely scratched the surface. On a visit to Bryce Canyon, my sister and I hopped into a ranger walk we saw going on. We hung to the back, walked along, and didn't expect to get too much out of it. A few minutes later, though, we were captivated. Ranger Poe was hilarious and smart and passionate, and I just remember thinking, "Man, I would love to be that guy." I continued to visit parks whenever I could, finished college, and got my first job as a seasonal ranger at Grand Canyon.

I am now working my second season with the National Park Service at Lassen Volcanic. Several years have gone by since that first trip out West. The connection I developed with these places is still burning today, and I feel so fortunate to be working for the Service that helps preserve and protect these iconic landscapes. I'm sure no matter what I end up doing in life, the national parks will always be a part of it. How lucky we are to have these places to escape to!

With the over 400 designations within the national park system, I hope everyone has the opportunity to get out and experience some for themselves. Whether it's a park, monument, seashore, or the National Mall, all have a ton to offer. And if you are able to step onto the trails or into backcountry, I encourage you to do so, and get to know these places a little deeper.

Lassen Landscape
Bonnie Wickliffe Adams
McBain, Michigan

When I was planning this quilt of Lassen Volcanic, I looked for a landscape theme that was unique to the park. I wanted to use the landscape technique I learned from fiber artist Gloria Loughman. I searched Pinterest for ideas and scenes and I was inspired by a photograph of the Painted Dunes by Chakarin Wattanamong-kol. Though the colors and composition are different from that photo, I think adding a variety of fabrics and textures gives more of a feeling of the outdoors. This quilt was made using cotton fabric and fusible appliqué with machine quilting.

Western Aster

Charla J. Viehe
Olive Branch, Mississippi

I grew up in Denver, always appreciating the views and the mountains, and throughout my life I have visited most of the parks. When I was ten, we visited a great aunt in California and one day we toured Lassen Volcanic. Learning that there was a steep trail to the top, I was determined to make it. In flip-flops, I climbed to the top of 10,463-foot Mount Lassen to see the spectacular view from the southernmost active, but dormant volcano. May 22, 2015 marked the centennial of the last great eruption from that mountain. The appliquéd footprint on this quilt is my actual current flip-flop pattern. The other footprints reflect my family getting out and enjoying nature in its amazing context.

I chose to make my quilt of the common western aster because I have been doodling wildflowers since I was a girl, and this is one of my favorites. Western asters, plentiful at Lassen Volcanic, can be found in a wide range of habitats. They are reminders that something does not need to be rare to be beautiful and appreciated.

Porcupine

Sandy Kretzer
Burke, Virginia

Quilts are texture, techniques, patterns, color, and process with a sprinkle of challenge. I enjoy experimenting with new construction methods and tools. I have very eclectic tastes in quilt projects. If only there were enough time to make at least one of everything.

Landscapes are new to my repertoire. An artistic teacher, talented quilting friends, and beautiful works by well-known quilters have lured me into making landscapes. I am especially interested in incorporating animals and plants with realistic details; there are many techniques and experiments on my to-do list.

This quilt was made using batik and traditional cotton fabric as well as ultrasuede. The porcupine quills are thin slices of fabrics layered, fused, and sewn together. I would like to thank my sister Bonnie Adams for painting the highlights on the eyes.

"*A multitude of animal people, intimately related to us, but of whose lives we know almost nothing, are as busy about their own affairs as we are about ours.*" JOHN MUIR

Located in central Kentucky; 52,830 acres
Established May 25, 1926
Official NPS website: www.nps.gov/maca
- The Mammoth-Flint Ridge Cave is the longest cave system known in the world
- Tours of the cave have been offered since 1816

Tricia Turcotte
Secretary, Office of the Superintendent

I am a veteran of the US Air Force, having served from 1992 to 1999. I worked in corporate America for thirteen years when my husband took a job in Kentucky in 2011. I began my new job search and thought maybe getting back into serving the American people would be a great place to start. My family and I have a great love for the beauty and history found in national parks. I grew up in Charleston, South Carolina, and frequently visited Fort Sumter and Fort Moultrie. These were the first parks I knew, and I fell in love with them. I spent some time in Denver, Colorado, where I was able to visit Rocky Mountain National Park. When I moved to northwest Florida, I had access to the Gulf Islands National Seashore and Canaveral. This is where my children first visited one of our national treasures. I was also able to incorporate a trip through Glacier National Park while serving a temporary duty to Montana. This was an absolutely beautiful landscape. I have worked at Mammoth Cave for over three years in this position. It is the best job I ever had because it is not a job to me. It is a passion and a lifestyle.

I have always been an adventurer and a lover of beautiful landscapes. My life in Kentucky satisfies my love for adventure at Mammoth Cave, where I witness some of the most beautiful and untouched landscapes. From the springs and waterfalls I find hiking in the woods to the dark and mysterious corridors in the cave passages, I have found home. The staff at this park brings another special attribute to working here. It is clear through their actions, words, and interactions with visitors and with each other the love they have for our resource.

My favorite spot at Mammoth Cave is actually in the cave. Gratz Avenue, off of the Historic Tour route, is filled with signatures of visitors on the walls made by slave guides almost 200 years ago. I could go through that passage for hours, and I always find something new. It intrigues me to see this still preserved and to follow the passages to places not visited by many. As for the time of year I most love, it's hard to choose between spring and fall. In the spring, the fawns begin to appear as the red buds start to bud. The spring colors in the grass and the blooms of the wildflowers are breathtaking. The spring wildflowers are stunning. One of my favorite places to see them is along the Cedar Sink Trail. As you get to the bottom of the "sink," large areas are covered with flowers named Jacob's ladder, shooting stars, and firepink. Several color variations of violets cover areas of the landscape as well. Spring wildflowers have never been so beautiful anywhere. In the fall, the warm colors start to appear as the leaves begin to change. The burgundies, browns, yellows, and some faint remnants of green on the landscape provide visitors and staff with great hiking and sightseeing opportunities.

There is no such thing as a typical day at this job, which makes this park that much more amazing to me. Because my primary job is to provide support for the Superintendent, I typically become involved in whatever she is working on. I love that my job isn't the same every day. Some things are similar daily: budget work, payroll, talking on the phone, for example. But as a rule, I could be in the cave with a visiting dignitary, in the woods helping one

of our scientists find or check on something, or working with a researcher on any number of citizen science projects happening in the park. It's an adventure every day!

There are many areas in the cave where water is found, which would make plenty of sense to most people, as caves are made by water. However, there are some areas of the cave where water is found that give us no indication of where the water comes from. The Science and Resource Management Division conducts dye trace tests to make that determination. This is a fact not widely known. Science fascinates me.

The most memorable of events since I have been here have been the Naturalization Ceremonies we sponsor in the cave. These are special times for the candidates who become Naturalized Citizens. There is no better or more unique way to become a citizen of this country than in one of its natural treasures, and in a cave. In 2013 a Naturalization Ceremony was held in the cave with support from a local county high school Junior ROTC. It was so fitting to have them there with us, celebrating life as American citizens, welcoming a group of new citizens. This was touching and exciting for everyone present.

Our national parks represent the best of America: our history, natural wonders, and resources, which, without proper care and preservation, would be lost to coming generations. From a history standpoint, we see the Washington Monument, the White House, the Statue of Liberty, Mount Rushmore, and more, and these are all so important to our history as a nation. There are also our preserved natural wonders such as the Grand Canyon, Mammoth Cave, and Yosemite, which share in our history. National parks are not just for recreation and enjoyment. They additionally provide educational opportunities and a glimpse into our history as a nation.

Mammoth Cave is one of the most beautiful and adventurous places one can visit. It is actually two parks: one above the ground, and one below. Exploring both is an experience not soon forgotten.

A Walk through Mammoth Cave

Barbara Dove
Alexandria, Virginia

My style of pictorial quilting represents an impression, whereby I capture a feeling or memory of a place. I am particularly interested in applying the art elements and principles used by artists, especially painters, to the textile medium of fabric and thread. My process is intuitive regarding color selection and I rely on my imagination quite a bit to design a quilt. I like to collage fabric; I rough cut and then place small fabric shapes next to each other to form an identifiable object. I call this style representational impressionistic collage. I also use symbols in my quilts to help create an emotion or to emphasize meaning.

Caves are dark, mysterious, magical, and delicate: impressions I wished to convey in my cavescape. I am taking you on an imagined walk through the three zones of a cave: light, twilight, and dark. Start at the upper left-hand corner with a sky hole, then go down the staircase and along a walkway. As you continue, notice many stylized cave forms, which I learned about in my research of Mammoth Cave. I have used some of the cave forms as symbols in this quilt. For example, calcite drips falling into a decanter-like stalagmite resemble tears falling from a face-like stalactite above. The face may have different interpretations, including a story about an ancient man who was killed in Mammoth while mining gypsum, a substance used for face paint. Other stylized cave forms allude to eternal life.

Hepatica

Janet Acuff Marney

Fairfax, Virginia

The cold winter is ending. Hidden deep in the forest, tiny wildflowers, smaller than acorns, push up through dead leaves and debris. Each little blossom has its cheerful color, perfect shape, and sparkling surface reflecting the sun's light. In the center is a noble crown of life. These are the first flowers of spring, symbols of resurrection and hope.

The woods are my place of peace. I depicted a woodland plant, hoping I might one day see it in person. I wanted to examine something often overlooked. After thorough research, I came upon some of the evergreen leaves quite by accident on a winter hike. I drew the liverwort leaf from my own photo. Using scraps discarded by others, I made a forest floor out of realistic dead leaf colors. At first, I found the drab look frustrating, but it became more and more satisfying as I layered different periwinkle fabrics with hand appliqué, machine appliqué, raw-edge appliqué, machine quilting, fabric paint, and ribbon, staying true to my vision. The final touch was hand embroidery and beading to make stamens.

Hepatica, one of more than 60 species of wildflowers at Mammoth Cave, is part of the buttercup family. Even the smallest plant shows the beauty of Creation, if we take the time to look.

Laura Robertson
Kearneysville, West Virginia

In this vivid underwater scene, we can see the bright red lure of the female freshwater mussel and the darter fish below, eyeing the bait. Freshwater mussels have a long and interesting lifecycle. Adult female mussels release small, larval mussels, called glochidia, that need to attach to a host fish as parasites, where they will feed for days to weeks before metamorphosis into juvenile mussels. The juveniles then drop off the host fish and settle onto a stream bottom, where some species may live up to a hundred years. Some adult female mussels develop elaborate lures to attract the host fish. Sadly, these fascinating animals are some of the most endangered groups of animals in the world. Mammoth Cave National Park is fortunate to harbor many different species of mussels, including several endangered species.

This quilt was machine pieced and quilted using commercial cotton fabrics.

> "Every rock temple then becomes a temple of music; every spire and pinnacle an angel of light and song, shouting color hallelujahs." JOHN MUIR

Betty Lieurance
Management Support Specialist

I began working for the Park Service at Rocky Mountain National Park in 1991. I initially took the job because it was available; then I discovered the NPS was where I belonged. I have been at Mesa Verde for almost sixteen years, first in human resources and now as a public information officer and management specialist.

Mesa Verde protects some very unique treasures. I especially enjoy Long House. This cliff dwelling doesn't attract as much attention as Cliff Palace, but I find it beautiful. My favorite season in the park is winter. I think the snow adds beauty to the scenery and the cliff dwellings. I love seeing bear, bobcats, and mountain lions.

I begin each morning thinking about what I need to accomplish. That plan quickly goes by the wayside when other things take priority. The busiest days in the park are Tuesdays and Wednesdays. It was memorable when two first ladies visited: Hillary Clinton and Barbara Bush.

I firmly believe we need to protect these treasures for future generations. I cannot imagine a world without a park to visit, whether it is a cultural park like Mesa Verde or a natural park like Yellowstone or Rocky Mountain. Equally important are those wonderful historical sites including Gettysburg, Ford's Theater, and Little Bighorn. Like most employees of the NPS, I bleed green!

I see a generation being raised with computers and information at the touch of a finger. I hope we can find a way for information on the computer to encourage people to get out and see the real thing.

Located in southern Colorado; 52,000+ acres
Established June 29, 1906
Official NPS website: www.nps.gov/meve
- The largest archeological preserve in the US
- The only cultural park in the national park system
- Created to preserve the cliff dwellings built by the Anasazi peoples

Cliff Dwelling

Mary Lois Davis
Austin, Texas

Growing up in Colorado meant studying the history of the state. In elementary school, over fifty years ago, I was fascinated to study the cliff dwellers in the southwest. I spent hours thinking about how these people lived in their "apartment buildings," nestled in the cliffs with sheer walls of stone above and below. These people hunted, farmed, made baskets and pottery. In short, they carved out a life in a difficult and rugged land. Many mysteries about the Pueblo people exist to this day, preserving the mystery surrounding the park. I finally was able to actually visit this amazing place, to feel the spirits of the former inhabitants, and continue to imagine life in Mesa Verde.

This piece was made using foundation piecing and raw edge appliqué.

The process of taking fabric and thread, cutting them up, and turning this into something completely different gives me great satisfaction and nurtures my soul. I use fabrics that are commercially produced, as well as some I've created using various surface design techniques.

On this piece, I made a background of machine-pieced squares on the diagonal. The flowers, stems, and leaves are made from hand-dyed fabrics, then fusible appliqué. I drew patterns, and cut out each shape individually. I continue to explore and create as this is an integral part of my being, and it brings me immense pleasure and satisfaction.

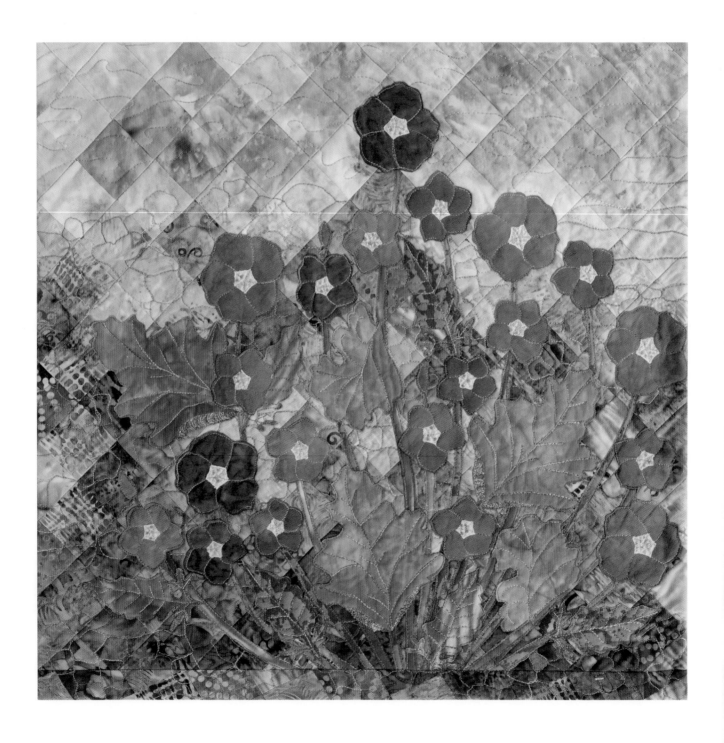

Collared Lizard

Gitta Smith
Burke, Virginia

In researching Mesa Verde for this project, I discovered the collared lizard. I was intrigued by its bright coloration and iridescent stripes. I love the teal color found in some of these lizards, and sought to accentuate it in my quilt. To create the yellow stripes, I hand-painted white tulle with yellow paint, then cut it into thin strips. The lizard and rock are machine pieced and hand appliquéd onto the machine-pieced background. I quilted the body of the lizard with iridescent, metallic, and variegated cotton thread in a sawtooth pattern to suggest the Pueblo Indian culture. Other parts of its body are quilted in similar Pueblo patterns.

MOUNT RAINIER

"Specimens of the best of Nature's treasures have been lovingly gathered here and arranged in simple symmetrical beauty . . . Its massive white dome rises out of its forests, like a world by itself." JOHN MUIR

Kathy Steichen
Chief of Interpretation and Education

Even as a child, when my family visited Mount Rainier, I realized this national park is a very special place; a place that I wanted forever preserved and protected. This passion led me to study park management at the outdoor recreation program at the University of Washington. During a family picnic, I first learned from a chance encounter with a park ranger about careers in national parks.

My work with the National Park Service began in 1975 as a seasonal park ranger at Mount Rainier National Park. I had just completed my sophomore year at the University of Washington, and found Ohanapecosh to be the perfect place to spend the summer. Since then my career has taken me to many parks and to two regional offices, but now I'm back at Mount Rainier.

Many people don't realize the diversity of careers that can be found in national parks. Mount Rainier hires people skilled at protecting park visitors, providing visitor information and education services, managing and researching natural and cultural resources (biologists, botanists, wildlife specialists, ecologists, GIS specialists), conducting business services (accounting, personnel, contracting, computer technology), and maintaining roads, trails and facilities (engineers, architects, carpenters, plumbers, electricians, road equipment operators).

There are many favorite places at Mount Rainier, but I find myself always drawn to the subalpine meadows surrounding the mountain. The majestic vistas of mountains and glaciers provide a perfect backdrop to delicate features of the wildflower meadows. It's fun to watch the hoary marmots, pikas, and other animals prepare, each in their own way, for the long winter ahead.

I always look forward to the season ahead and I watch for the beacons of change. As the snow begins to melt each spring, brilliant yellow skunk cabbage brighten the moist areas of the lowland forest while avalanche and glacier lilies sprout through the snow in the high country. Colorful subalpine wildflower meadows display a sequence of flowers, ending in the late summer with the incredible blue of the mountain bog gentian. As fall brings changing colors, an early snowstorm may momentarily cover the meadows, reminding us that winter is just around the corner.

Pikas are fun to watch! They live in rocky talus slopes, in subalpine parts of the park. During the summer they collect grasses and other vegetation for their winter food. Pikas do not hibernate, but dig tunnels underneath the snow to travel between their different plant caches. The pika's distinctive short, high-pitched call is usually heard before they are seen.

In addition to being protected as a national park, Mount Rainier is a Wilderness Area and a National Historic Landmark District. This district, designated in 1997, recognizes the National Park Service rustic architecture, a design using massive logs and glacial boulders as building material, best suited for integrating structures with their natural setting. The historic buildings, bridges, and rock walls all contribute to the special character of the park.

National parks are places where memories are made and stories begin. Mount Rainier is an icon to the natural beauty of the Pacific Northwest. While my personal memories and stories are many, my most exhilarating memory was the first time I stood atop the mountain. As an avid hiker, but not a climber, I pushed myself to both my physical and emotional limit to reach the summit of Mount Rainier. It's a two-day climb and on the second day you leave the high camp in the middle of the night with only a headlamp to guide your steps. Gradually the starlit sky and faraway city lights give way to the first light of the day. Watching the dawning of the new day while traversing the glacier to the mountaintop was an experience I will always cherish.

National parks preserve spectacular landscapes, natural and cultural resources, wilderness, stories, and memories. These living laboratories and historic museums are truly the fabric of our nation.

Above Myrtle Falls
Lynn Chinnis
Warrenton, Virginia

I love mountains, and knowing that we would spend the summer in Washington, I was delighted with the opportunity to depict Mount Rainier. I took many photos during our two days in the park and decided to try a more realistic work than is usual for me. Since our visit was too early to see the wildflowers, and Mount Rainier is known for its flowers, I took the liberty of adding some to the meadow, based on a photo my husband took on a visit several years ago.

Lupines

Donna Marcinkowski DeSoto
Fairfax, Virginia

I aim for realistic work in my art quilting, but sometimes creating a quilt that looks just like a photo, which looks just like the real thing, is something I don't want to attempt. Instead, striving for a more abstract portrayal, I put hundreds of little fabric pieces of blues, purples, periwinkles, and greens together to give an impression of the stunning sense of beauty I felt, upon finding myself in a field of endless lupines at Mount Rainier.

This reverse appliqué is a technique by Beryl Taylor. I have done several different pieces this way and find joy and peace in putting a broad assortment of fabric together, stitching crazy, uneven curves, and then snipping away layers to reveal the surprises underneath. Although there is some tedium involved in this technique, the repetitive layering, stitching, and snipping is soothing and meditative.

Mount Rainier is formidable from the air. The time my family spent there exploring the trails, trying to spot elusive pikas and taking in the glorious sights, which included lupines, is something I will never forget.

Mountain Goat
Angela Laperle Miller
Palmyra, Virginia

After seeing Mount Rainier and gaining some understanding of the remote and inhospitable terrain, I find it remarkable how the mountain goat lives and raises its young at such high altitudes. I was inspired to create a mountain goat as part of the mountain. With grace and dignity, he watches over and protects this land he calls home. He is monarch of his mountain.

Swirls, twirls, and curls have always attracted my attention. On fabric or with thread, these shapes give my imagination a place to take hold. From this evolves a story to tell. I try to express a moment in time, and to show gratitude for it.

NORTH CASCADES

Located at Washington/Canada border; 684,000 acres
Established October 2, 1968
Official NPS website: www.nps.gov/noca
- Home to 300 glaciers and 300 lakes
- Holds the record for the greatest number of plant species recorded in a national park

"Down the long mountain-slopes the sunbeams pour, gilding the awakening pines, cheering every needle, filling every living thing with joy." JOHN MUIR

Rosemary Seifried
Wilderness Ranger

I have worked nineteen years as a wilderness ranger, beginning as a volunteer with the Student Conservation Association, and now as a supervisor for the wilderness information center. Because I have a strong love of wild lands and a real desire to serve the public in a meaningful way, working for the National Park Service was a perfect fit. I grew up in New York but I had no idea there were so many glaciers in Washington State. I had to see it for myself, and once I did, I never left.

Golden Larches from Easy Pass in fall is a highlight for me. The sea of peaks from Sahale cannot be missed. It is true beauty to behold, and always makes me feel peaceful. My favorite season is autumn, hands down. The cooler days reduce the bugs, bring out the colors, and it all makes for perfect hiking weather. The air smells so good—the river, the drying leaves—you can always smell when fall is in the air.

A typical day in our office is jam-packed helping people plan trips to the wilderness—climbers, boaters, backpackers, and day hikers. Rangers help folks plan trips, issue permits, explain the current conditions and Leave No Trace, and so on. It can be very hectic, but it's always great to work with folks who are so happy to talk to a real ranger who knows the park, and to see folks excited about the area they are about to visit.

I absolutely love weasels and wolverines. I have been lucky enough to see a weasel from time to time in the wilderness, and it is always memorable. I know there are wolverines in the park, but I have never seen one. There is still time, however.

Author Jack Kerouac once spent a summer here as a lookout on Desolation Peak, in 1956, and used part of his experience in his book *Desolation Angels*. The lookout is now historic, and folks like to hike to it and see where Kerouac spent time. The NPS still uses it for a fire lookout.

We need the tonic of wilderness to survive, now more than ever. Although the National Park Service cannot preserve everything, it does try to preserve the very best of our natural and cultural heritage. All Americans should be able to experience these places, and the only way to do that is to protect these areas and steward them carefully.

Everyone plays a role in this, not just the Park Service. I love to visit other national park sites myself, because even if I don't know much about an area, if I see that it's a National Park Service site, I know that something interesting happened there. I encourage all to approach their national parks with an open mind and a willingness to learn and experience something special. You will not be disappointed.

Spring Morning at Mount Shuksan

Pat Washburn
Chantilly, Virginia

In 1973, I moved to Fort Lewis, Washington. To someone from Kansas, the mountains were special. Hiking in the Cascades was an enjoyable treat. On my first hike, I arrived at a crest on the trail, looked up, and gasped at a pristine vista, with glacial mountain peaks, shades of vermilion trees, pops of magenta alpine flowers, and a cerulean blue sky. It was quiet, almost like a church. Breathing the crisp air saturated with evergreen fragrance, I knew I was not in Kansas anymore.

I started my quilt by looking at my old photographs and viewing the North Cascades website. I gathered memories and drew this scene, placing Mount Shuksan in the middle. Knowing of the tall waterfalls in the area, I placed one to the side of the mountain, like a close-up. Reliving my first encounter in the Cascades, I drew myself with long hair, 1970s bellbottom jeans, and a sweater coat, throwing my funky hat in the air with the excitement of the view.

I transferred my drawing to fabric, then painted the sky and water. I added fabric and more paint, used markers for detail, and oil pastels for shadows. Free-form flowers jump out of the foreground. I finished the quilt with both hand and machine quilting.

Since that time, I have visited many national parks and continue to be grateful for the opportunity to see the grandeur of our beautiful country.

Bracken Fern

Rose Rushbrooke
Portland, Oregon

This art quilt is a fractal representation of the bracken fern, which covers vast areas of the North Cascades. The fern is a branching structure and it exhibits randomness and variation at each level. The plant is an example of a self-similar set. This is a mathematically-generated pattern that can be reproduced at any size.

Fractals are self-repeating patterns describing nature and infinity. Brought to the attention of the public by the late mathematician Benoit Mandelbrot, these quirky formulae are considered an interesting subset of modern geometry. The iterated equations may answer many universal questions. The ability of human beings to make sense out of chaos is an endless source of fascination. Why are we so drawn to these images? Are we hard-wired to see fractals? If so, why, and what are they telling us?

Construction of this quilt followed basic principles of quilt making: batting sandwiched between backing and a pieced top, with the three layers quilted together. I work with printed cotton, my own hand-dyed fabrics, shibori, cotton and silks, and other manmade and natural fabrics. My work is done by hand, using needlework tools, and a sewing machine. Being in immediate contact with the materials adds to the pleasure of creation.

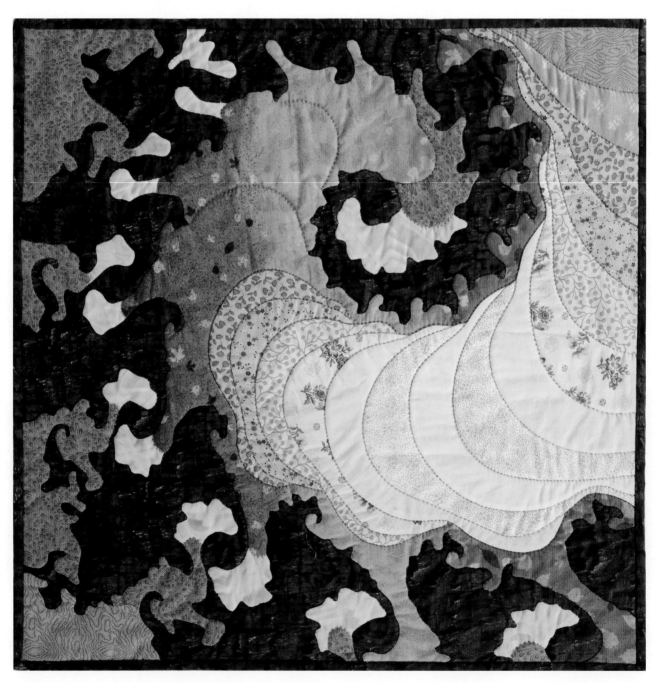

Pika

Kim K. Gibson
Burke, Virginia

The pika, *Ochotona princeps*, is a "marker species." It informs us of the health of the tundra and environs. Cute and engaging, not too shy, but rare enough to thrill us when seen, the pika is a reminder of our responsibility to serve as wardens and guardians to this world and its many denizens.

OLYMPIC

Located in coastal Washington; 922,650 acres
Established March 2, 1909
Official NPS website: www.nps.gov/olym
- Includes four distinctly different ecosystems
- Mount Olympus gets more than 200 inches of precipitation each year, mostly in the form of snow

"The tendency nowadays to wander in wildernesses is delightful to see. Thousands of tired, nerve-shaken, over-civilized people are beginning to find out that going to the mountains is going home; that wildness is a necessity; and that mountain parks and reservations are useful not only as fountains of timber and irrigating rivers, but as fountains of life." JOHN MUIR

Barb Maynes
Public Information Officer

I decided I wanted to work in national parks when I was thirteen, during a family trip through the Southwest. A ranger at the Grand Canyon took the time to share his favorite stories about the park and helped me understand what made it such a special place. By the end of the trip, I knew I wanted to have the same kind of job. Since then, I've worked in nine different national parks, and each one has been a dream come true. I have worked at Olympic for twenty-five years.

There's so much variety that there is always something fun, new, or interesting to see or do. If I'm in the mood for sweeping mountain vistas, there are glacier-capped mountains. If I'm looking for a quiet walk in the woods, there are towering centuries-old forests. Or if a beach sounds fun, there are rocky beaches and sandy beaches, plus craggy offshore rocks and islands.

I love the Hurricane Hill trail. In summer, it's a great place to find mountain wildflowers in bloom, and on clear days, the views of the Olympic Mountains and Strait of Juan de Fuca are spectacular. If it's really a clear day, I can even see glints of the Pacific Ocean.

The Olympic Mountains have been isolated from the rest of Washington's mountains for millennia,

in the past by glacial ice, and today by the water and lowlands. As a result, there are plants and animals that are endemic, unique to the Olympic Mountains and found nowhere else on Earth. In the high country, one of my favorites is the Olympic marmot—it's one of the species of animals that's endemic.

The largest dam removal in US history happened within Olympic between 2011 and 2014. Part of the Elwha River restoration project, the dam removal has freed the Elwha River, allowing salmon to return to the upper Elwha after an absence of over 100 years. Restoration of the salmon runs and the entire ecosystem is in full swing now, and visitors can see the process as it unfolds. To learn more about this project, check www.nps.gov/olym/learn/nature/elwha-ecosystem-restoration.htm.

National parks protect the places that tell the story of our country and its people. These include landscapes and ecosystems that are unique in the world. And they include places where uniquely American people and events have occurred, from Independence National Historic Park, where both the Declaration of Independence and the US Constitution were signed, to the birthplace of Martin Luther King Jr., to the Manzanar internment camp where Japanese-Americans were held during World War II. These places are preserved and protected so that we, and future generations, can visit, learn, wonder at, and find our own connections with the places and the stories they tell.

Breathing Green Air at Hoh Rain Forest

Regina Grewe
Kamen, Germany

I consider quilts as textile landscapes: mountains and valleys in vibrant colors, enhanced by additional magical light sparkles on which the light conjures additional effects. I love walking through nature, breathing fresh, cool air, leaving behind everyday life and simply "being," enticed by the path to discover new sights and striking details. Enjoying nature this way generates a very special, balanced mood, which I long to take home and preserve in a quilt.

Re-creating the manifold appearances of nature as straight lines and shapes is a challenge that I gladly take on. The trickier the graphical and technical undertaking, the more intensely I try to find new solutions and possibilities leading to an elegant result. With a little bit of luck, the memories and feelings will be found in my finished piece. And if the quilt transmits a glimpse of that feeling to the viewer—perfect!

My preferred technique is paper piecing, so for this project a detailed layout was absolutely necessary. I used a selection of images to explore the natural textures in detail and to develop a design that could be pieced. My computer, with a variety of special drawing programs, is the most important tool to create these precise drawings.

This quilt reflects memories from long hikes during the spring at the Hoh Rain Forest in Olympic National Park. I was especially fascinated by the endless shades of green found in the leaves and moss; the reflections created a green shimmer in the wonderfully green air. How refreshing it was to take a breath! The National Park System not only preserves the fantastic natural landscapes, but also makes them accessible to visitors. I am personally thankful for this, because it would have been impossible for me to hike and enjoy the woods without the paths and trails. That is the reason I placed a hiker on a footbridge in my scene.

Fungus

Laura Espenscheid
Austin, Texas

I love national parks. A lifelong dream of mine is to visit every one, and I am thirty-one percent of the way there; I have a spreadsheet. We spent our wedding day at Glacier National Park before heading to the Justice of the Peace.

Several years ago, we planned a visit to the Seattle area. We spent most of the trip hiking on the Olympic Peninsula. I fell in love with the plant life surrounding us, especially the colorful fungi growing on the tree trunks. I knew as soon as I saw this fungus I would one day turn it into a quilt.

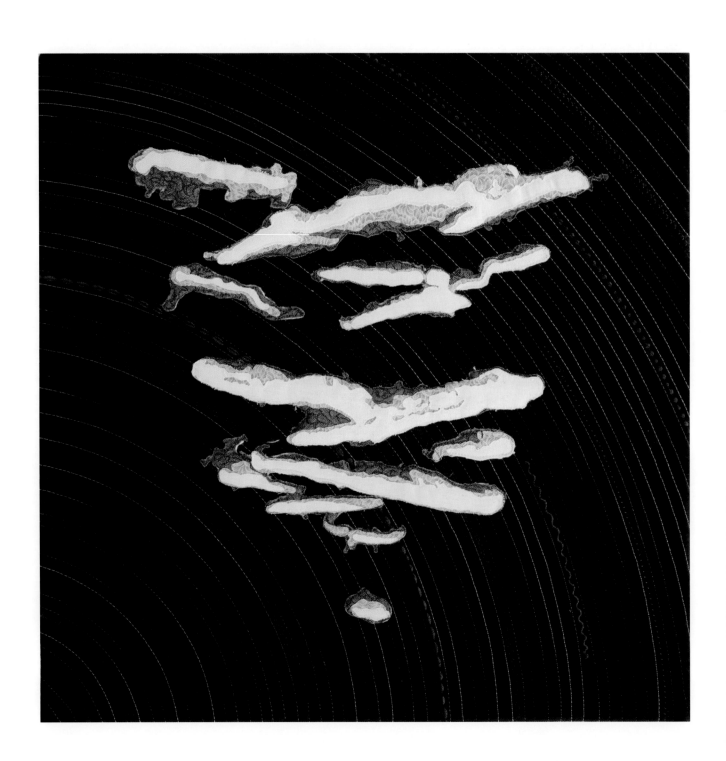

Surf Smelt

Donna Marcinkowski DeSoto
Fairfax, Virginia

The park called Olympic is nothing short of spectacular. I loved the time I spent with my family in this park, especially at Lake Crescent and at Rialto Beach. Right away, when I read about the surf smelt that visit the waters of Olympic en masse, the smelt called me. I am the daughter of a fisherman. I can still remember times living near Port Huron in Michigan, and living near Turnagain Arm in Alaska, when exciting news came that the smelt were running. Off ran my Dad, with my brother and any of the other menfolk he could wrangle along to cast their nets in the night and dip into the bounty. What always ensued the next day was a most delicious fish fry, thanks to Granny and Mom.

It can be rewarding to complete a 20-by-20-inch piece of fiber art using hundreds or thousands of bitty pieces of fabric and a riot of stitching to actualize an art quilt. (I know this to be true, because it is how I constructed the other quilt I made for this project.) But there is something beautiful in economy: economy of materials and time. To make this quilt, I needed water, a fabric that would show the gorgeous blue of the Pacific Ocean, and then I needed a completely different kind of fabric that would convey the surface of a shiny, silvery, slippery, skinny little fish. After making simple sketches of the fish, cutting them out, and placing them in an appealing array, all this piece needed to be complete were some gently curving lines of stitching to convey the water's movement around the fish.

PETRIFIED FOREST

"Nature is not so poor as to have only one of anything." JOHN MUIR

Hallie Larson
Park Ranger, Interpretation

I grew up between Yosemite and Kings Canyon/Sequoia National Parks, and spent a great deal of wonderful family time at these and at many other national park sites. Between those special times and my parents' knowledge and concern for conservation, my return was inevitable after becoming a research biologist.

For seventeen years, I've been an interpretive park ranger at Petrified Forest. This park is beautiful and has many facets: the semi-arid grassland, the ancient Triassic fossil deposits, and a human history over 13,000 years long. My favorite characteristic of the park is that it is a living laboratory. We continue to actively survey the park and discover new fossils, learn more about the complex geology, delve deeper into the archeological heritage, and explore the vital current environment.

I usually list four basic spots that are musts for our visitors, but Blue Mesa probably is my personal favorite. It is a sculptural, eroded fantasy of blue, purple, pink, and gray sedimentary rock from which large fossil logs emerge. In the spring there are flowers that bloom at Blue Mesa that I haven't encountered anywhere else in the park. The paleontology of Blue Mesa is very rich as well, and includes giant Triassic amphibians and delicate fern fossils.

Located in northeastern Arizona; 218,000+ acres
Established December 8, 1906
Official NPS website: www.nps.gov/pefo
- Route 66 passes through the park
- A Spanish explorer is rumored to have named the area "El Desierto Pintado" (the Painted Desert) due to the colors of the sunset.

All of our seasons are dynamic and fascinating in their own way, but I most enjoy autumn for nice temperatures, less chance of big storms (including dust storms), and there are the last flowers of the growing season, such as golden buckwheat. The crowds are also smaller, which gives visitors a chance to wander a trail on their own.

Our work schedule is varied and we all share the different shifts, which keeps things interesting. The shifts change throughout the year as visitor needs fluctuate. One of my favorite shifts is going into the park in the morning to walk Puerco Pueblo trail, amidst the remnants of an ancient village. I respond to questions, initiate conversations about the site and park, and give impromptu interpretive walks through the archeological site. After that I might return to the visitor center so other staff get a lunch break, and I give information and orientation to visitors from all over the country and the world. That can be a very busy and intense time, but it is also fun to help visitors best enjoy the park. The rest of the day I am perhaps stationed at Painted Desert Inn National Historic Landmark, an absolutely charming Pueblo-revival style building perched on the rim of the Painted Desert. With its organic curves, hand-painted glass skylight, and Hopi murals, the Inn represents the history of the region—and the nation—during the first half of the twentieth century and a bit beyond. The stories of the people linked to the building include homesteaders, different Native American cultures, Civilian Conservation Corps, and the Harvey Girls. The travel corridor is still in use from the railroad through the National Old Trails Highway and Route 66 to the Interstate. Depending on the time of year I might be treated to the sight of sunset on the Painted Desert as I close the Inn. It is a fun and fulfilling day for me, given the many opportunities to be helpful to visitors.

For years there were rumors of all the petrified wood being taken away and that there were strict rules making it difficult to come and visit. This is simply not true. There are massive and medium sized logs all over the various "forests" of the park; the ground is littered with small and miniature pieces, like a carpet of gems in places. The park is great to explore and discover both on maintained trails and also off-trail. We want people to go out and see the amazing amount of petrified wood and other beautiful resources we have here. As erosion exposes more, and our researchers subsequently discover new things, it makes for a very exciting place.

Because of my background in biology, I love our current environment. While many of our animals are not seen by the average visitor due to timing, we have numerous and diverse species of fauna: pronghorn, mule deer, coyotes, foxes, bobcats, golden eagles, bullsnakes, collared lizards, rufous hummingbirds, tarantulas, pallid bats, ravens, red spotted toads. The plants entrance me. At first glance, Petrified Forest doesn't seem as green as home. Once visitors begin to observe the landscape, they realize that it is a quilt of different shades of green: silver, teal, celadon, mint, forest, hunter, and all the rest. The plants have adapted to a demanding environment, yet they still have delicate and lovely blossoms in a kaleidoscope of colors. Part-of what I do is take photos during the blooming season to share on the park's various social sites for Wildflower Watch. My favorite? Tough to pick just one, but I'd probably have to say a dramatic milkweed called antelope-horn with baseball sized green and maroon flower clusters.

Among the many interesting happenings here at Petrified Forest, I especially like that we had a visit from Albert Einstein in 1931, John Muir explored the area in 1904 to 1905, and in 2004 President George W. Bush signed a bill authorizing expanded boundaries for Petrified Forest National Park, more than doubling the size of the park.

The parks for me represent the highs and lows of our history, the best of our amazing beauty and complex landscapes, the richness of our natural resources, and the diversity of our cultures. The parks are a welcome to visitors from afar and they are love notes to the future. They are oases for all of us, to remind ourselves of these things, but to find solitude and thoughtfulness as well. I am so very proud of our parks and my coworkers and partners for being able to share this legacy.

I have worked in a dozen parks; all are unique, each with different stories. The parks are America: good, bad, beautiful, poignant, and thrilling. They remind us of the past, bring fun and joy today, and are a voice to the future. Petrified Forest National Park is ever changing, but also preserves and protects aspects to enhance experience and understanding of often abstract and difficult themes. In the end, it is also just perfect for sitting on a rock and listening to the song of a wren, while contemplating our place in a vast landscape.

Painted Desert
Meggan Czapiga
Bethesda, Maryland

Geology, gems, and fossils have always fascinated me. Their beauty, colors, and textures appeal to my inner artist whereas their creation, over millions of years, appeals to my inner scientist.

I constructed the base of my quilt using batiks in colors typical of the geology found at Petrified Forest. I added fancy yarns to represent the vegetation in and around the park, and the crystals and beads suggest the permineralization of the forest. For the backdrop for the park, the Painted Desert, I was inspired to use twisted bugle beads in many shades and sizes to accentuate the stratified layers of siltstone,

mudstone, and shale. These fine-grained rock layers contain abundant iron and manganese compounds, which provide the pigments for the various colors of the region.

Much of the Painted Desert region is within the Navajo Nation. The number four plays an important role in traditional Navajo philosophy, and is symbolized by the four appliquéd soaring eagles. I incorporated this spiritual component because the natural landscape is so vast and beautiful.

Evening Primrose

Cheryl Rounds
Vienna, Virginia

The evening primrose blooms at Petrified Forest in the evening; I chose to portray this flower on my quilt. Creating quilts gives me a blank canvas to express how colors, fabrics, and threads convey and reveal personal emotions. Thanks to the fabric manufacturers, the quilt is stamped in time, leaving a picture of the world's view of life for a short period in history.

My enjoyment of color in the natural environment has allowed me to use fabric colors to express my appreciation for how nature combines many variations of colors.

Western Meadowlark

Lois Sovey
Herndon, Virginia

Sometimes I get the urge to hold a needle and thread. There is something so satisfying about manipulating fabric. I especially enjoy hand appliqué, and I found this project very challenging. All the fabrics came from my stash including that of the background grasses, which I thought was perfect to highlight the meadows in the Petrified Forest National Park. Unable to find the perfect fabric for the meadowlark's wings, I fussed with the construction and finally pieced each feather individually. I'm still unsure about the result but I don't believe I'd change anything if given a do-over.

I would like to credit Joseph Sovey for the bird design I used to make this quilt. I machine pieced, hand appliquéd, embroidered, and hand quilted this piece.

PINNACLES

Located in central California; 26,000+ acres
Established in 1908 as a national monument; redesignated on January 10, 2014, by President Obama
Official NPS website: www.nps.gov/pinn
- The newest national park
- Pinnacles are rocky spires remaining from an ancient volcanic field
- Best wildflower viewing is March through May

"And the stars, the everlasting sky lilies, how bright they are now that we have climbed above the lowland dust!" JOHN MUIR

Jan Lemons
Chief Ranger

I have worked at this park, in this job, for almost a year. Before Pinnacles, I worked in concessions at Rocky Mountain National Park while I was in college and I fell in love with that park. Pinnacles has all of the things I love about the parks: hiking, climbing, caving, bats, bobcats, and a horse program. This is a small park and I know all of the staff; they are so dedicated and committed to their work.

What I like best are the waterfalls in Bear Gulch Cave. They are seasonal, unique, and ever changing. My favorite season here is the fall when the weather starts to cool down and we prepare for the busy spring season. I think the bobcats here are really neat. They are very mellow and just like to hang out and watch what is going on. Most people don't know that we have over 400 species of bees at Pinnacles. If you visit mid-week, the park is empty.

Every day at my job is different. Some days I do paperwork, others I help fight wildfires, educate or assist visitors, and protect visitors and the resources. I work together with the local communities; there is a lot of variety. Our administrative officer just retired after having worked here for thirty-two years. She was great to work with and so knowledgeable; seldom do employees work that long in one park.

Pinnacles is a small gem in the middle of a bustling area. All should come out and enjoy a hike, an evening program, or a picnic.

Denise Louie
Former Chief of Natural and Cultural Resources Management; currently at the NPS Pacific West Regional Office

I worked at Pinnacles for a little more than nine years. I have a passion for working in national parks; it is a good mission to be a part of, and I believe in what I am doing.

Pinnacles is a hidden gem. It has long been underestimated and undervalued by those who have never visited. You can't drive by and understand what this park is all about. You have to get out of the car and into the environs. Although not too far from large urban centers, it is rural and real. The park's surrounding areas are private working landscapes and they are compatible with upholding natural and cultural riches of the region.

I am particularly drawn to the Balconies Cliff and Balconies Cave areas. In a short hour and a half hike, visitors enter what seems to be a completely different world from the east side of the park. It is a super scenic area. I like the fact that a road was never built connecting the two areas, which has maintained Pinnacles' rustic nature. The days are longer and the nights are cooler from late spring through late fall. During the summer, evenings, nights, and early mornings are glorious. It is always pleasantly cool and the dark nights reward visitors, who can see more stars than they knew were up there. Soak in this place with all of your senses.

Roadrunners, tarantulas, and canyon wrens bring me the taste and memory of many years I have spent in the desert. I enjoy badgers. They are everywhere, but you are lucky if you ever see one. California condors are special. All effort needs to be made to eliminate their biggest threat for survival: lead. When feeding on animals that have been killed, condors inadvertently ingest fragments of lead in spent ammunition, and they can become poisoned this way. Outreach and education will hopefully result in non-lead ammunition.

For the first time in a hundred years, Pinnacles has begun developing relations and a working partnership with indigenous tribal people. These efforts have influenced and enriched park stories and understanding.

Chapparel and Spires at Pinnacles
Christine Vinh
Arlington, Virginia

My inspiration for this piece came from my niece, Charlotte Law, who lives in California and has hiked in Pinnacles. When I heard about this project, I asked for some of her pictures, which I used for inspiration in designing the quilt. The materials, techniques, and hand stitches were chosen to highlight the colors and textures of the trees and rock formations Charlotte captured in her pictures. I used an especially wide variety of materials, including hand-dyed silks, burlap, cheesecloth, cottons, batiks, silks, hand-spun yarn, hand-dyed vintage lace, hand-painted silk, and embroidery threads. Techniques include raw-edge machine and hand piecing and quilting, appliqué, stamping, and embroidery.

Shooting Star Flower

Shoshana Spiegel
Herndon, Virginia

When I make art, sometimes I paint, but mostly I quilt. The intuitive painting process is spontaneous and requires no planning. I just need paper, brushes, paint, and a willingness to let go of the expectation of a product. With quilting, the appeal is the texture, the pattern, and the color of the fabrics. I feel a chemical connection that is exciting, especially when I consider which fabrics to use together. I like the predictability of the project design and outcome, and the challenge of planning the construction methods.

I was intrigued when I first learned of this funky flower with such interesting shapes and colors, the long stems with a cluster of leaves way down at ground level. I spent too much time drawing the composition. Making the flowers was the fun part. It was surprisingly difficult to find the shade of pink I wanted. Combining the colors while ensuring enough contrast with the background was the challenge.

This is one of the flowers that blooms earliest in the year at Pinnacles.

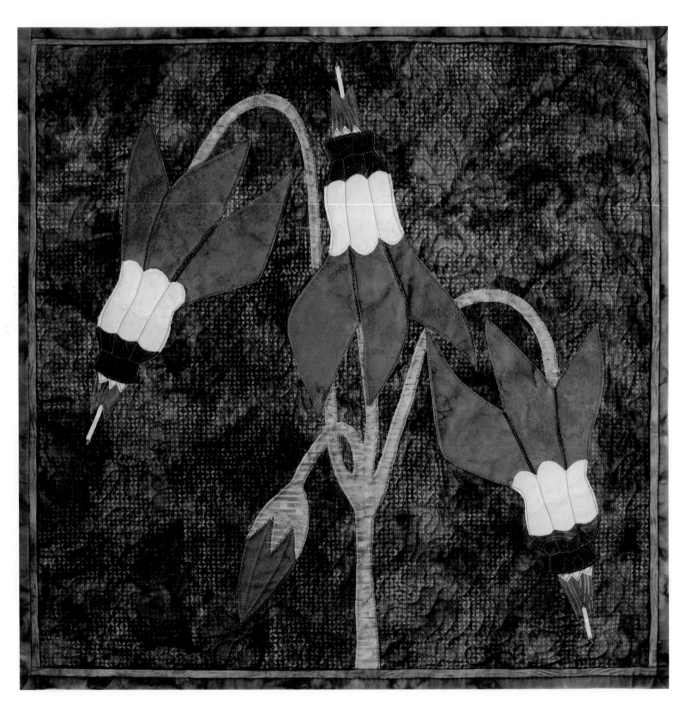

Violet Green Swallow

Judy Anderson
Fairfax, Virginia

To try and create the beauty of this bird in fabric was fun and exciting. This is one bird I would love to see in person. Someone told me that the colors in my quilt are spot on. Beautiful birds definitely add to the remarkable landscapes of our national parks.

I used cotton prints and batiks to make this quilt with raw-edge appliqué and thread sketching.

REDWOOD

"Any fool can destroy trees. They cannot run away; and if they could, they would still be destroyed . . . God has cared for these trees, saved them from drought, disease, avalanches, and a thousand straining, leveling tempests and floods; but he cannot save them from fools,—only Uncle Sam can do that." JOHN MUIR

Located in northern-coastal California; 131,983 acres

Established October 2, 1968

Official NPS website: www.nps.gov/redw

- The oldest living coastal redwood is at least 2,200 years old
- Redwoods are the tallest trees on Earth

Mike Poole
Park Guide

I have been here since 2007, initially as a park volunteer, then for four years as a seasonal interpretive ranger. Since 2012, I have staffed the public information office. I wanted to be a park ranger since I was in junior high school; I am now sixty-one.

Redwood is no different than any of the other major national parks, in that the parks are special because they preserve the best that America has to offer. Redwood forests are an amazingly beautiful ecosystem that needs little explaining. In addition to the redwoods, Redwood National and State Parks also protect and preserve the associated ecosystems to keep the forest healthy. The park is diverse. It is fifty miles long, and is full of favorite areas. My favorite part is the little pocket beaches that form between points of land and jut into the ocean. I love the Enderts Beach trail hike to the tide pools. My favorite Redwood experience is driving the Howland Hill Road and walking the Stout Grove. During the winter rainy season, it is quiet and peaceful. When wet, the bark of the trees darkens and changes colors. I especially like the sound of the rain moving through the tops of 300-foot tall trees.

Did you know there is more biomass in a redwood forest than anywhere else in the world, including the Amazon rainforest? Redwood trees are 300 feet tall or more; they are immense. At the end of World War II, before there was this national park, patriotic groups across the country donated enough money to buy 5,000 acres of redwoods as a thank you to the soldiers who fought the war. The 500-year-old or more trees, which have endured combat with nature and survived, were a fitting tribute to the men and women who fought. Today, that grove survives as the National Tribute Grove.

National parks preserve the best that America has to offer. They are to be protected so we can enjoy them today, but also so they will still be around for our children and our children's children long after we are gone. Almost daily, people call this park to tell me Redwood National Park is on their bucket list. I think the redwoods are a part of the collective soul of America. This park belongs to each and every one of us. I encourage everyone to visit at least once in your life.

Tall and Majestic

Beth Marshall Meenehan
Fairfax, Virginia

My husband and I took our then three-year-old son to the Redwood National Forest, and I was amazed by the splendor of those massive trees. A small quilt cannot do credit to their immensity, but it was exciting to try. Somewhere, in my mass of photographs, I have a picture of little Marty and me, at the base of one of those ancient wonders. We stood by the tunnel that went into the tree. We were dwarfed by the enormity of the hole through which cars were driving. Above the tunnel, the tree went up and up and up; we couldn't see the top.

This is the first art quilt I have made that involved this much thread-painting. It was a lot of fun to make, but it took about five months to complete. I have no idea how much thread it took. A lot. And I have no idea how many stitches there are. A lot. The thread painting on the trunks of the redwood trees was done in layers to provide texture and color. The tops of the trees are more abstract but given the lack of one's ability to see the tops of such tall trees, it is less noticeable.

I appreciate Kyoko Yamamura for doing the binding and sleeve for this quilt.

Trillium

Lesly-Claire Greenberg
Fairfax, Virginia

I begin each quilt with a color palette and an idea, sometimes with just one special fabric. I use solid colors and prints, but my favorite is hand-dyed cloth. I collect from artists who sell the fabric they dye. I experiment with various printing processes and add paint to highlight parts of some designs. Using surface design techniques this way allows me to put my own stamp on my art.

The petals and leaves of the trillium were each made individually; the flower was constructed independently of the background, and applied to the dyed background after it was completely bound. After washing my fabric in the washing machine, I collected the remnant loose threads and formed the flower center.

The second-most popular hike at Redwood, Trillium Falls Trail, was named for these beautiful flowers growing in the park.

Roosevelt Elk

Polly M. Davis
Warrenton, Virginia

I am constantly learning and I thoroughly enjoy the process of figuring out how to maneuver fabric and stitch it into the form I envision. Starting out with an idea of what I want my quilt to look like becomes a struggle with my sewing machine in an attempt to come close to my original idea. I love the process of deciding how much of what kind of handwork I need to employ to enhance what I am able to do with the machine.

Combining colors, shapes, and textures with fabric to create a visual story is such joy.

An elk with seven tines to his antler is referred to as "imperial." With this in mind, I wanted this fellow, the Roosevelt elk, to be regal and to drip with jewels to indicate he is the ruler of his territory. This largest of the elk species was named in 1897 in honor of Teddy Roosevelt. How fitting a tribute for a man who, as president, preserved wildlife refuges and millions of acres of forests, established national monuments, and doubled the number of national parks. He was known as our great conservation president for good reason!

ROCKY MOUNTAIN

Located in north-central Colorado; 265,770 acres
Established January 26, 1915
Official NPS website: www.nps.gov/romo
- This park contains the Continental Divide and headwaters of the Colorado River
- It licensed the first female nature guides in 1917

"We are now in the mountains, and they are in us, kindling enthusiasm, making every nerve quiver, filling every pore and cell of us." JOHN MUIR

Barbara Scott
Interpretive Park Ranger and Centennial Coordinator

The mission of the National Park Service, to preserve and protect for future generations while allowing for enjoyment, is truly selfless. When I tell people about the national parks and about the special resources they contain, I feel like I am doing my part to make the world a better place. That is why I work here, and I have been employed at Rocky Mountain since 2011. All of the parks are special to me, but the mountains here are captivating.

The alpine tundra is the most spectacular part of this park. It is a beautiful, unique ecosystem with sweeping panoramic views that survive the harshest of conditions. Rocky Mountain is one of the few places like this that can be easily accessed by car. Fall is my favorite season here; the trees change color, the elk are in rut, and the weather is spectacular.

Rocky Mountain is one of the few national parks established before the National Park Service. We get over three million visitors per year. It is also ninety-five percent designated wilderness, so if you take the time to hike a few miles, you'll find yourself in an amazingly pristine and quiet wilderness.

I love our flowers! We have an incredibly diverse assortment of wildflowers that explode in the summertime. You can take a short hike and find beautiful fields of wildflowers of every size, shape, and color. I'm also a big fan of the pika, a small rabbit-like alpine resident who spends the summer scurrying around, gathering vegetation to survive the winter. They are very cute.

Memorable things happen in the park every day. Some of these things are joyful, some are tragic, others revolve around families, solitude, or adventure. The reason parks mean so much to people is because of the memorable events that every visitor has in them.

National parks embody our history, our heritage, and our future. They remind us of all the pieces, happy, sad, beautiful, and ugly, that have made us who we are. They ground us, and they elevate us.

Rocky Mountain National Park is within a short drive of the huge population of the Colorado Front Range. Although we have so many visitors, we can still celebrate the beauty and peace of these mountains. It remains as pristine, and even more protected, than it was 100 years ago when the park was established. It shows the will of the American people to protect and preserve a special place that could so easily be overrun. The people created it through grassroots campaigns, and the people will continue to preserve it for future generations: a true testament to the mission of the National Park Service.

First Snow

Barbara Hollinger
Vienna, Virginia

High clouds set against a clear blue sky follow the first snowfall in the high mountains, marking the change of the seasons. Below the majestic peaks spread lush beaver valleys, highland meadows, stone-filled streambeds, and steep hillsides streaked with golden aspen. The diversity of Rocky Mountain National Park makes it truly a glory to behold.

Aspen

Nancy L. Evans
Jeffersonton, Virginia

This art quilt depicts golden leaf aspen trees, inspired by a trip to the Rocky Mountains in the fall.

I began with needle-turn appliqué and have added new art techniques, such as thread play, inking, and collage to my repertoire. With the freedom to spend time designing and sewing, I love every quilt project I begin in my studio. From drawing the design, to stitching on the label, each step to completion has its own special satisfaction and reward. I thank my husband, Steve, who gave me wonderful advice during the construction process of this original design, which helped me to be successful.

Mountain Lion
Catherine Kane
Fairfax, Virginia

I still have a vivid mental image of a mountain lion I saw at the Denver Zoo a few years ago. He was such a magnificent creature! He deserved to be recreated in vibrant reds and golds and royal silks.

My fiber art is particularly inspired by a sense of place. I enjoy collecting images, both mental as well as those represented by my photos and sketches, as I travel in the US and abroad. At home, I translate these images into full-scale cartoons and then select colors and textures of fibers and other materials that will help me recreate the sense of place.

Mountain lions, also called pumas, cougars, and panthers, are the largest predators at Rocky Mountain National Park.

SAGUARO

Located in southern Arizona; 91,327 acres
Established March 1, 1933
Official NPS website: www.nps.gov/sagu
- This park hosts more than 1.6 million giant saguaro cacti
- The area is home to six species of rattlesnakes

"Others, standing as erect as bushes and trees or tall branchless pillars crowned with magnificent flowers, their prickly armor sparkling, look boldly abroad over the glaring desert, making the strangest forests ever seen or dreamed of." JOHN MUIR

Andy L. Fisher
Chief of Interpretation

When I was in college studying forestry, I was granted an internship with Arches National Park. I knew I wanted to do something outdoors, but I wasn't inclined to work in commercial forestry. The internship introduced me to the best career I could have ever imagined. I have been working at Saguaro since 2008.

Saguaro National Park is a special place because Saguaro cacti are our nation's icon for western adventure. You can't think of the American southwest and not picture a Saguaro cactus, yet they are incredibly unique and fragile. Saguaro cacti can live to approximately 200 years, and often don't put forth their first branch until they are seventy-five or older. In addition to the cactus, we also protect one of the largest sky island ecosystems as wilderness. Where else can you live in a city of one million people, wander out of your backyard, and into protected wilderness? Tucson is very unique in this way and I love it.

My favorite spot at the park is Manning Cabin. At 8,000 feet, this historic log cabin was built in the early 1800s. It is nestled into the ponderosa pines of the Rincon Mountains. Once the summer residence of a former Tucson mayor, it is now a backcountry ranger residence.

Choosing a favorite season at the park is hard for me; it is a tie. We have five seasons here: winter, spring, first summer, second summer and fall. Spring for us starts in February, and by March, the wildflowers are a riot of color on the landscape. Second summer begins in mid-June and is when our monsoon rains begin. Between the Saguaro fruit ripening, and the rumble of thunderstorms cooling off our scorching days, I do love monsoon season.

The National Park Service is here to protect our national story. Who we are as a nation and the path we took as a society to get here is preserved in the 400-plus national park sites that are set aside for this and future generations. Our history is inseparable from the places where it happened and continues to happen. There is something at Saguaro for everyone.

Mountain Vista
Elizabeth Richardson
Alexandria, Virginia

This quilt represents my impression of the Saguaro National Park area. What I remember most from my visit there were all the cacti, the open sky, and distant mountains. My husband's photographs inspired this composition.

Saguaro

Jane M. Brown
Burke, Virginia

Although I find the living saguaro cactus majestic in its own right in scale and simplicity, my favorite form is the dead saguaro cactus. It gives an artistic vibe to the landscape, and its inner core is exposed in mighty splendor.

My interpretation of the dead cactus began with a piece of faux leather, overlain with strips of synthetic suede for the bones of the cactus. The strips were couched with embroidery thread. I used ribbon to give dimension to the trunk. The cactus arms are covered with layers of silk cocoon and woven stringy thread mesh. The background is from a piece of purchased hand-dyed fabric I found at a quilt show.

Roadrunner

Bobbie Dewees
Springfield, Virginia

I graduated from Arizona State University and visited Saguaro National Park several times. Arizona is where I saw my first roadrunner and truly learned the meaning of the phrase "hot enough to fry an egg on the pavement." This version was done as a joke one weekend when I was not feeling well, in response to a friend's advice to "think outside of the box." I was truly expecting to do a serious version later, but the ladies in my Playgroup quilting bee loved this one, so what could I do? I have a dry wit and love to throw subtle humor into my art quilt work whenever I can.

Sequoia	Kings Canyon
Located in eastern California	**Located** north of Sequoia National Park in eastern California
Established September 25, 1890	**Established** October 1, 1890
Official NPS website: www.nps.gov/seki	**Official NPS website:** www.nps.gov/seki
⚜ Home of the General Sherman Tree, the largest living single stem tree in the world (275 feet)	⚜ The area containing sequoia trees (approx. 15,800) covers 3,100 acres

"The dullest eye in the world must surely be quickened by such trees as these." JOHN MUIR

Colleen Bathe
Chief of Interpretation, Education and Partnerships

During the summer between eighth and ninth grades, I participated in a special Wider Opportunity Girl Scout Camp at Ten Sleep, Wyoming. As a pre-trip we visited Yellowstone and Grand Tetons National Parks. We hiked, camped, and participated in ranger walks, talks, and evening programs. Before we finished this trip, I had decided I wanted to become a National Park Service ranger. I don't remember seeing any female role models doing this. Still, it didn't occur to me that I couldn't do it.

I am in management, so I spend a lot of time in meetings, helping to make decisions about funding, or working on facility improvements and special events. I supervise eight people and meet with my staff. I write reports and grant proposals. I enjoy helping the staff; as a manager, I need to provide them with the support and tools they need to do their jobs. In turn, they take care of the visitors.

Since beginning this job, I have made a point of backpacking for ten to twelve days a summer. The scenery is spectacular, and I love the granite! In the wilderness of Sequoia and Kings Canyon there are many special places. It requires some effort to get there, but I really like Cloud Canyon and Deadman Canyon. For places to drive to, Mineral King and Cedar Grove have outstanding views. Winter is my favorite season here; I love the contrast of snow with the giant sequoia trees. I like to tell people that the limbs on the giant sequoias are bigger than most trees in other parks. I like watching the acorn woodpeckers outside my office window.

In the 1980s, the park began the removal of structures that were built on the roots of giant sequoia trees. This was a bold move, as many generations of visitors stayed in the campgrounds and cabins in the Giant Forest. Now, people return to see the resilience of the forest and reminisce about their childhood visits. Visitors can use the free shuttle to move around the Giant Forest, leaving their cars parked.

Sequoia National Park was established as America's second national park. We celebrated the 125th anniversary of Sequoia in 2015. We celebrated the seventy-fifth anniversary of the majestic park Kings Canyon in 2015.

Note: These two parks are geographically contiguous, but are administered separately by the National Park Service jointly as the Sequoia and Kings Canyon National Parks. Together, they comprise nearly 900,000 acres.

Mount Whitney and the Giants

Rosanne Williamson
Warrenton, Virginia

The challenge in making this quilt was perspective. I needed to show the size and grandeur of the sequoia tree and the beautiful vista of Mount Whitney in a vertical quilt. The scene came together with the addition of western dogwood blossoms.

As a quilter, I seek challenge. Whether through technique, design or interpretation, I want to grow as an artist with each project. I challenge myself to use new and innovative ideas, combined with traditional quilting skills. I share the sisterhood of finding art in fabric, pattern, color, style, and fine workmanship. I honor the skill and talent of generations of women, including my own grandmothers, who used this medium for function and beauty.

Fivespot
Sandi Goldman
Annandale, Virginia

The fivespot flower is one of many beautiful wildflowers found in Sequoia National Park. I've had the opportunity to explore and enjoy this park and I am honoring it with my interpretation of this flower. We should not take this gift of our national parks for granted.

On my daily walks I often stop to take photos of flowers and trees in my neighborhood. I see beauty in the infinite color combinations, textures, shapes, and patterns found in nature. I will never run out of inspiration from this amazing Earth we inhabit.

This is a wholecloth quilt, hand painted and hand quilted.

Ladybugs
Karin Tauber
Blacksburg, Virginia

Most of my art begins with traditional blocks, exact seam allowances, mitered borders, and hand appliqué. I combine these with art techniques, like raw-edge machine appliqué, extensive machine embroidery and thread-work, and overlays of tulle and organza for shading and depth. Free-motion quilting enhances the design, and beading adds sparkle and increases the dimension. In the quilting world, there are traditional quilters and free-form art quilters. I like to describe myself as a traditional art quilter.

I first came upon migrating convergent ladybug beetles on a hike through Capulin Volcano National Monument in New Mexico. It is a truly astonishing sight to see thousands of little red bugs clustered around the stems of trees and bushes, covering the bark so completely that it becomes obscured. Ladybug adults migrate to the mountain canyons in late May, feeding on aphids and pollen, to tide them over their nine-month dormancy. Congregating by the thousands, they overwinter in tight aggregates under fallen leaves or bark in many forested areas, Sequoia National Park among them. The warmer days of spring wake up the little critters, which initiates several days of mating. Then they begin their return migration to the valleys and fields to lay eggs and begin a new cycle of life.

It was important for me to create a tight cluster of ladybugs as well as one ladybug I've named Isabella. She is the large ladybug ready to take flight, opening her red wing covers to unfold her intricate flying apparatus. Being the first one to leave, she looks a bit nervous.

I enjoy the unique challenge of making realistic landscapes. I experiment with different fabrics, paints, and mediums to make them appear 3-D. I have traveled frequently since my retirement from federal service, mostly visiting national parks on the way to various conventions. My visits provide many beautiful photos to create a quilt scrapbook of my travels. I was excited to participate in this project and hope to visit more of the parks in years to come.

Sacred Datura

Pam Shanley
Radford, Virginia

I was overjoyed to be able to use beautiful white fleece, wool felting, machine quilting, and hand embroidery to depict this wonderful plant. Everything fell into place to complete the idea.

Sacred datura, sometimes called jimsonweed, is part of the milkweed family, and is found at Kings Canyon.

California Quail

Teresa Bristow
Springfield, Virginia

While attending quilt shows, I quickly discovered my favorite section is the pictorial and landscape quilts, especially those including wildlife or nature scenes. I wasn't sure I had the skills to create such beautiful pieces, but ideas began to grow and cook in my mind. I came to learn this is part of the process. When all the pieces finally do fall in place, it may be very different from the original concept, and it's often better.

I especially enjoyed this National Parks project. This challenge and the beautiful artistry of others have given me some wonderful ideas for future projects.

The California quail is one of many local species that live at Kings Canyon year round.

SHENANDOAH

Located in western Virginia; 200,000 acres
Established May 22, 1926
Official NPS website: www.nps.gov/shen
- Just 75 miles from Washington, DC
- Includes 101 miles of the Appalachian Trail
- Home to the scenic Skyline Drive

Matt Graves
Chief of Interpretation and Education

A combination of people and experiences led me to my "life's work" with the National Park Service. My dad was trained as a survival instructor during his time in the US Air Force, and he shared his outdoor knowledge with his sons. We camped as a family, thus nature and the outdoors have always been a part of my life. Both of my parents grew up on farms and I was lucky enough to be able to spend time on those farms as a child. John Denver music, Jacques Cousteau TV specials, and *National Geographic* magazine all took me to places I could barely imagine, growing up in rural North Carolina. All of these things, plus backpacking on the Appalachian Trail, rock climbing, and canoeing, led me to a job with an organization that was all about the outdoors. Since I grew up during the environmental movement of the 1970s, I saw the clear need to protect the environment and all that lives in it. I have worked in my current position at Shenandoah for nearly four years. This is the thirteenth National Park Service site I have been lucky enough to work at!

As chief of interpretation, every day is different. Some days I work with my colleagues on complex management issues: air quality, invasive or endangered species, resource protection, or visitor services needs and details. Some days, I work with the interpretive program managers in planning school programs, new interpretive exhibits, or training for frontline park ranger/interpreters. Since we are close to Washington, DC, Shenandoah receives many visits by international conservation professionals from around the world. They come here to learn how the US National Park Service manages its protected lands and cultural resources. I participate in numerous meetings on budgets, administration, purchasing, and human resources. All of these areas have behind-the-scenes impact on the management and protection of this special park. My job certainly isn't boring!

Shenandoah is one of the largest fully protected natural areas in the entire mid-Atlantic region of our nation. No hunting, resource extraction, or consumptive use is allowed. As much as possible, nature reigns here. Unlike in the West and in Alaska, Shenandoah is among a handful of unique natural national parks east of the Rockies. Seeing visitors experience the more than 500 miles of trails and nearly 200,000 acres of nature (80,000 acres of which is also congressionally designated wilderness) so close to tens of millions of Americans is something for us all to be proud of.

Although most of the large western national parks were carved from public lands, Shenandoah was created from privately owned land. By the time the decision was made to establish eastern national parks in the "western tradition," most eastern land was already highly settled and in private ownership. If Virginia wanted a national park in the northern Blue Ridge, the state had to acquire the land and then donate the land to the federal government. Today's park looks like a large natural landscape, but in reality, the entirety of Shenandoah has been previously used for farming, grazing, timber, mining, growing orchards, hunting, and gathering. Most everyone, except for the keen observer, misses the fact that nature has been restored in Shenandoah.

For me, there is no single favorite spot in Shenandoah. Every place is different, depending on when you're there; the season, time of day, weather, and whom you are with all make for varying experiences. As a park manager, I don't get to spend nearly enough time actually out in the park, so I really enjoy being in uniform at places with park visitors. Answering their questions, sharing my knowledge, and helping them have meaningful experiences make every place in the park a favorite! On my own time, I enjoy hikes with my wife and our dog on the numerous dog-friendly trails uniquely found at Shenandoah. What could be better than being with family outdoors in a beautiful and natural setting?

While all of the seasons are unique, and we do have four distinct seasons here, I love the quiet and stillness of winter. As Shenandoah is ninety-five percent covered with an eastern deciduous hardwood forest, winter is a time when summer's green curtain is pulled back and you have an opportunity to see the landforms and all that is hidden during the lush green of the summer season. The crispness that comes with cold, clear days adds to the pleasing experience of winter in Shenandoah.

Shenandoah is home to a diversity of plants and animals. It's hard to pick out one plant or animal as a favorite, without bringing attention to the habitat in which it lives. We have rare plant communities on the highest peaks in the park; there are high elevation wetlands, too—Ice Age relics. Black bear and bobcats abound with the food and shelter they need to survive. Over 200 species of birds use the park at some point during their life cycles. We even have native brook trout thriving in the clear, cold and clean water, protected within the park's numerous watersheds.

It is my hope that my staff facilitates memorable experiences for our visitors every day. We strive to help our visitors find and discover something special for themselves every time they visit Shenandoah.

Almost every aspect of American ecology and geology, history and recreation culture (including the good, bad, ugly, and controversial), wilderness and recreation is represented in one of our national park sites. They are places where we can directly experience an environment, historic landscape, ecosystem, or built environment very similar to a past time or in a manner where natural processes are allowed to run their course. Parks also allow us to study the evolution of our nation's land ethic and of the conservation movement. So much of our world has been modified to meet humans' needs, but national parks preserve a picture or a movie of a static or changing story.

There are 407 individual units of the national park system today, spread all across the country and our territories. While each park was established for a specific reason or story, most of our parks tell multiple stories and offer something of interest for everyone. As we approach the centennial of the National Park Service and move into the second century of protecting our national treasures, my hope is that all Americans and our visitors from other nations will get out and experience our national parks. A visit to a national park can literally change your life; I've seen it happen.

Skyline Drive

Vivian Milholen
South Riding, Virginia

My designs are inspired by nature. Whether it's the burst of a brilliant sunset or the new leaves of a spring day, each piece depicts a memory of nature. Using my camera and a sketchbook, I capture the blankets of color I see emerging from the brown foliage or the trees, reaching to the sky.

I use a collage technique, cutting organic shapes from fabric, to recreate woodland scenes. I often use paint and

ink to enhance the design. After the design is finished, I stitch the layers together with various colors of thread to create the quilted texture of the composition.

Rhododendron

Hollis Olson
Lovettsville, Virginia

The outdoors fascinates me. I am happiest when I am able to re-create on fabric or other materials scenes or objects I observe in nature or in my travels. Photography plays a large role in my design process and helps me to remember details that I otherwise might have forgotten.

I love being a fiber and mixed media artist because it affords me the opportunity to be creative, while combining the love of fabric, photography, and nature. This quilt is adapted from a photograph I took while camping in the spring at Big Meadow Campground in the Shenandoah National Park. The small amount of wool I used was from sheep from Loudoun County, Virginia. It was dyed in the microwave. I "snow dyed" some of the fabric used for the rhododendron petals; this is a process where fabric is placed under a layer of snow and dye is added on top. As the snow melts, the dye migrates, creating mixing of colors on the fabric.

Red Fox

Debra Woodworth Godwin
Winchester, Virginia

A photograph taken by a close friend served as the starting point for this quilt. Once an idea begins to take form, determining how to execute the project is a global rather than linear process for me. In my imagination, a quilt is fully formed immediately before the first tangible act occurs. The conundrum is manipulating materials to conform to the imagined design. The creative process of working with my hands, pulling fabrics and threads from my stash, and moving a quilt beneath the presser foot of my sewing machine results in rapidly firing neurons and increased dopamine levels and ends in sheer delight, satisfaction, and exhaustion. My art is primarily for me.

Thank you to Gail Felice, The Crossings, Bloomery, West Virginia, for taking the photograph that inspired this quilt.

Located in western North Dakota; 70,446 acres

Established April 25, 1947 (authorized as a national memorial park; redesignated in 1978)

Official NPS website: www.nps.gov/thro

- Cannonball concretions, formed by selective precipitation of mineral-rich groundwater, can be found along the North Unit Scenic Drive
- This park is split into two unconnected pieces

"A fruitful day, without measured beginning or ending. A terrestrial eternity. A gift of good God." JOHN MUIR

Andrea Markell
Park Ranger, Interpretation

I've spent three winter seasons here as a park ranger/naturalist. This is the first national park my parents took me to as a kid. I grew up in North Dakota and this was a favorite getaway. When I was three years old, we camped in the campground, and I remember my dad waking me up to see a bison scratching his chin on the picnic table, right outside of our camper van.

My favorite spot is the Riverbend Overlook in the North Unit of the park. This park is a great place to see wildlife. Unfortunately, during the westward expansion of the 1800s, many species were extirpated from the Great Plains. The National Park Service reintroduced bison, bighorn sheep, and elk to the park, creating a refuge for the wildlife. Of the national parks, Theodore Roosevelt said, "We have fallen heirs to the most glorious heritage a people ever received, and each one must do his part if we wish to show that the nation is worthy of its good fortune."

Kate Sedlacek
Park Ranger, Interpretation

I have been here just over a year. I began as an intern in the summer, and by winter, became a park ranger. My favorite place at this park is Wind Canyon/Boicourt. Once you come to the end of these trails, you are on the edge of a butte looking out at the badlands (the badlands is a barren area where soft rock strata have eroded into varied shapes). This provides an amazing bird's eye view of the landscape.

We have one of the largest concentrations of petrified wood in the US. Our petrified wood consists of trees one normally finds in swampy environments like the Florida Everglades. This interesting fact provides a glimpse of how geographically diverse the badlands are. My favorite flora in the park is sage. There is a lot of sage throughout the badlands and the most amazing smell arises after a rain shower has come through, while the sage dries off in the sun.

Theodore Roosevelt is commonly referred to by visitors as a hidden gem of the National Park Service, for good reason.

View of My 50th State
Stevii Graves
Leesburg, Virginia

My friend Cathy Norell and I spent several days at the park in Medora, North Dakota, envisioning what it must have looked like when Teddy Roosevelt was there, riding his horse and hunting bison. No Interstate freeway was there, to be sure, but still, wide open spaces, and creamy brown everywhere, were only interrupted by bright blue skies. I used a variety of techniques to capture the image of the park from my photograph. The image looks stark, but I know there is an active ecosystem going on that is not evident.

I grew up traveling a great deal because we moved often. A few years ago, when I decided to make a list of the states I had visited, I was surprised I was only missing one, North Dakota. I think I saved the best for last. Visiting the Teddy Roosevelt National Park was the frosting on the cake.

Coneflowers

Sarah Entsminger
Ashburn, Virginia

In the grasslands at Theodore Roosevelt, one of the most well-known flowers growing in the wild is the *Echinacea angustifolia*, the lavender coneflower. This flower is prized not just for beauty, but also primarily for medicinal properties. Native Americans with access to the root of this plant used it to help with a wide variety of illnesses. Echinacea is still widely used as an herbal remedy today. Native echinacea species are dwindling due to heavy harvesting of the roots to serve the herbal pharmaceutical industry. This species is a protected plant within this park.

My quilt was created using a wide variety of quilting cottons to illustrate the grassland background. The coneflowers were made with ultra-suede, felted wool, embroidery, and beading. I used ink to create the subtle coloring in the sky.

Bison

Jennifer Weilbach
Littleton, Colorado

I took the photograph for this in 2001 as we did a northern sweep from a soccer tournament in Minnesota back to Colorado. Upon seeing the picture, my sister exclaimed, "You are never allowed on an African safari—the animals would eat you alive when you got so close." I almost didn't tell her the picture was taken from safety inside the car window, with my husband's foot ready to accelerate if this bison even thought about standing up. Yes, I was about six feet away.

Editor's note: The park warns that bison can become agitated and charge without warning. "Always view them at a distance and give them the right-of-way if encountered on the road ... be patient, stay in your vehicle, and observe them quietly."

VIRGIN ISLANDS

Laurel Brannick
Education Specialist

I have worked at this park since 1992. I have been a lifeguard, ranger, and education specialist and now am a supervisor. I work here because when I moved to St. John, I wanted a job where I spent time outside. Virgin Islands National Park keeps St. John beautiful. The park comprises fifty-six percent of the island. Many people don't realize the park boundary goes out into the water. This is a unique place where visitors are able to see healthy corals, fish, marine life, clean beaches, undeveloped tracts of forest, birds, and other wildlife.

My favorite spot is Francis Bay. There is also a nice salt pond where you can view birds. The beach is beautiful and sea turtles and rays abound. This area has the highest concentration of wildlife of any other spot in the park.

My favorite season in the Virgin Islands is spring because there are not as many tourists at that time and the water is warm. Migratory birds are plentiful. I work in the visitor center, lead hikes, and work with schoolchildren. I lead walks every Friday and I enjoy showing visitors how to spot birds.

Our park was the location of the 1733 slave revolt. The story was made into a TV show called *Moments in Time*.

The Virgin Islands National Park has it all: natural resources as well as cultural resources including incredible views, beaches, coral reefs, wildlife, and ruins and petroglyphs from the past.

Located on the island of St. John in the US Virgin Islands, southeast of Florida; 7,000+ acres
Established August 2, 1956
Official NPS website: www.nps.gov/viis
- Bats are the park's only native mammal
- This is the only place in the US where driving is on the left side of the road

Trunk Bay

Sarah Entsminger
Ashburn, Virginia

Trunk Bay is arguably the most visited location within the park and is enjoyed by thousands of visitors each year. In addition to the gorgeous beach, Trunk Bay includes a well-marked 225-yard-long underwater snorkeling trail. The trail provides an amazing view of the underwater habitat of the island.

This double quilt represents two landscape views of Trunk Bay. The top quilt shows one of the most captured views of the Bay, as visitors swim and relax in the shallow waters. It was created using a variety of cotton fabric, paint, and ink. The construction methods were machine appliqué, piecing, quilting, and painting. The bottom quilt illustrates the underwater snorkeling trail. It was created using a wide variety of threads on a silk background. It is machine quilted as a whole cloth quilt.

Heliconia

Anne Argentieri
Fairfax Station, Virginia

I chose to depict the flora heliconia from St. John's because I was in the mood to make a tropical quilt. I love the color and clarity of the water in the Caribbean. I wanted to use vibrant colors in my quilt, with a touch of my favorite color, purple. Kyoko Yamamura's quilting enhanced the water and the flowers.

Loggerhead Turtle

Jeanne Coglianese
Fairfax, Virginia

While snorkeling off the coast of St. John, I saw my first sea turtles. They swam slowly to the surface and then back down again, unlike fish, which swim often in the same plane. In depicting this turtle on my quilt, I wanted it to appear as if it was swimming back down to the depths of the Caribbean Sea. I selected the beautiful blue and green batik fabrics to reflect the colors of the Caribbean, and found other batiks to show the subtle colors of the turtle's body and shell.

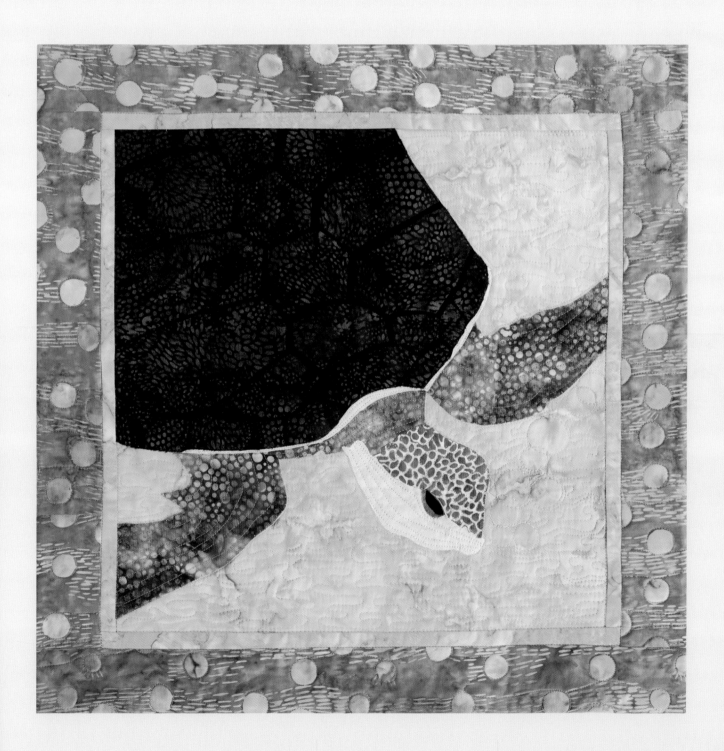

VOYAGEURS

"The forests of America, however slighted by man, must have been a great delight to God; for they were the best he ever planted." JOHN MUIR

Tawnya Schoewe
Chief of Interpretation

I have been at Voyageurs since 2001; I began as a district interpreter overseeing the year-round visitor center. I decided to work for the National Park Service because I believe in what it stands for, and I wanted to be a part of that.

This park is water-based. Most people don't know the water all flows north to Hudson Bay. The tranquility and solitude a visitor can find here is everywhere. Autumn is my favorite season. The leaves have turned, the bugs are almost all gone, the air is crisp, and it is just plain beautiful at that time of year. I am partial to the pines in the park. There are red pine, white pine, and jack pine. They are beautiful and some even tell the history of the past: fires, logging, recreation.

Voyageurs is truly amazing in so many ways. The rocks tell the story of the heart of the continent. The bedrock that makes up North America, and the fact that there are no roads into the park, are incredible and it is a wonderful challenge to experience.

The parks are all unique and they each have their own story. They tell about America either in a natural landscape vision story or in a cultural resource story. All people need to do is listen to the park speak. Everyone hears something different.

Located in northern Minnesota; 218,000+ acres
Established January 8, 1971
Official NPS website: www.nps.gov/voya
- 40% of this park is water
- In winter, the surfaces of the park's lakes freeze up to two feet thick

Landscape of Voyageurs

Patricia Scott
Edmonton, Alberta, Canada

Colors and textures found in nature inspire me. I enjoy using commercial patterns and I also design my own. Pushing the limits with my own unique art quilts is my real passion and where I find the most angst, as well as the most satisfaction. My art expresses exploration of my own boundaries, which I always challenge. I tend to charge ahead, not fully knowing the path my work will take, but enjoying the journey to the result. I am encouraged and inspired by artists of many mediums.

To make this quilt, I followed a method by Gloria Loughman.

Blueberries

Katherine W. Heslep
Alexandria, Virginia

When I went camping in Voyageurs, I was amazed at the expanse of water. It is certainly the dominant presence in this park. But on land, I was delighted to find wild blueberries. They taste more intense than the cultivated ones. They are smaller and lower to the ground, so it is a humbling experience to forage for them, making them all the more special on a hot summer day.

I wanted to convey the beauty of the shrub in all seasons: winter branches, delicate, pale, bell-shaped blossoms touched with pink, berries in various stages of ripeness, and the brilliant scarlet fall foliage. The blueberry fruits are so tiny in comparison to the main visual of the water, but no less important as a food source for many creatures.

Special thanks to Dr. Kerry Britton, plant pathologist, who cut out the winter bush on this quilt and certified that it was free of pathogens, and to Andrea Harles who helped by cutting out the bell-shaped blossoms.

Loon

Andrea L. Harles
Washington, DC

Lakes and the wildlife around them have always been a vital part of my life. I remember my first trip to a national park at age four with my grandparents and great-grandmother and aunt. We went to Voyageurs. I especially remember the experience of wilderness and the time we spent in the boat fishing. There are said to be about 150 breeding pairs of loons in the park, and I was eager to depict one of them. We have a rustic camp on a small lake in Maine where we adore seeing and listening to loons.

I used a photograph taken by my husband of a loon on our lake as the basis for my quilt. I stripped it down to essential lines and colors using Photoshop. My goal was to convey some of the mystery and ancient qualities of both the loon and the wilderness of the park.

WIND CAVE

Located in western South Dakota; 30,000+ acres
Established January 9, 1903
Official NPS website: www.nps.gov/wica
- This cave is the first to be designated as a national park
- Winds have been measured at the cave's entrance at over 70 mph

"Winds are advertisements of all they touch, however much or little we may be able to read them; telling their wanderings even by their scents alone." JOHN MUIR

Josh Nelson
Park Guide

I have worked a total of four seasons at Wind Cave in the division of interpretation. This involves staffing the visitor center, leading five different cave tours, and presenting surface programs and environmental education programs for kids of all ages. One reason Wind Cave is special to me is this was the first park where I was able to wear a "flat hat": the iconic hat of a park ranger.

I love that Wind Cave seems to always hold a surprise for people. Many visitors don't realize the extent of the cave, or that the park offers over 30,000 acres of mixed-grass prairie and ponderosa forests to explore. Visitors are excited at the opportunities to view bison, elk, pronghorn, and other animals. Although each season is unique in its own way, there is nothing more majestic than sitting out on the rolling hills of the park at sunset during the fall and listening to a bull elk bugle. There is a huge contrast between the winter and summer at Wind Cave. Summer days are filled with leading multiple tours a day and staffing information or ticket desks. During the winter the visitation drops, which allows more time for environmental education groups and project work, such as podcasts. Regardless of the season, my responsibilities always focus on the visitor experience.

Many people don't realize when they arrive that Wind Cave is still a frontier. Despite being one of the longest explored caves in the world, Wind Cave is probably even longer. The current map of 143 miles is possibly only ten to fifteen percent of the overall size. This estimate is generated through measuring the wind that blows in and out of the cave's small natural entrance.

Because of their small size, occasionally prairie dogs are overlooked. But really, who can deny that communities of yipping "dogs" are adorable? If you take even a few minutes to understand them, you begin to realize this is a creature the entire structure of the prairie is built upon. Many animals prefer grazing on the short clipped grasses in the prairie dog towns. The prairie dogs also provide habitat for some creatures, and are a food source for others. You don't have to be large to be mighty.

Recently the park acquired 5,556 acres. In addition to providing more acreage for bison, elk, and other animals calling Wind Cave home, it contains a site believed to be a prehistoric bison jump. Bison jumps were rugged steep drops or small cliffs the Native Americans would drive the massive animals over. Then they would use the animals for food, clothing, and tools.

Imagine for a minute the country without the parks. What would that change? Think about traveling to Grand Canyon or Yosemite Valley if they were not parks. Left in private or corporate hands, would they be different? National parks teach us about ourselves through the past, which is our history, and they can be seen as an investment in the future, ensuring open, undeveloped areas remain that way.

Boxwork Showing Stalagmites How to Hold Stalactite

Dolores M.G. Goodson
Lovettsville, Virginia

July 2001 was my month of national parks and monuments. Our family of four visited over eighteen amazing sites. We drove from our home in Virginia, northwest to Montana, south to the Grand Canyon, and back. When given the opportunity to create something from cloth and thread inspired by a favorite experience, I jumped at it.

This quilt was born from that trip and my husband's carpentry skills, as that is the first thing I thought of when I saw the amazing formation on the ceilings of Wind Cave.

Free piecing, appliqué, paper piecing, free-motion quilting, and hand quilting were all employed to create a family memory.

Fairy Ring Mushrooms

Maggie Ward
Warrenton, Virginia

Fairy ring mushrooms are so named because they have a central spore (mycelium) that sends out shoots in all directions, each with a mushroom at the end. The mushrooms appear in a ring. Not surprisingly, these rings have long been fodder for many folktales and superstitions.

My fairy ring is placed just outside a very small opening in the cave wall. The viewer, who is apparently also very small, is in the cave, looking out at the night sky. The mushrooms glow, providing their own magical light. Although a search of the Wind Cave website did not reveal the presence of fairies in the park, it also did not say definitively that there were none. Viewers are invited to make their own interpretations of that omission.

Red-Tailed Hawk

Laura C. Gilmartin
Stafford, Virginia

Red-tailed hawks can be seen at Wind Cave along the Lookout Point and East Bison Flats Trails.

My dad always used to point out the hawks in the woods around his home and on various trips to run errands. When he could no longer drive, I would take Dad to his doctor's appointments. At one particular curve in the road, he would say, "I always stay in the right lane and go slow because this is a dangerous curve." On the day of his funeral, coming home from the service, there was a hawk on a telephone pole, on the right side of the road, at the most dangerous curve in the road. Until then, I had not seen a hawk perched there. Dad worked construction throughout his life, and his nickname was "Red." I took this as a sign that the red-tailed hawk was meant to be my quilt for this challenge. When I am missing my dad it seems all I need to do is look around, and I'll see a hawk.

WRANGELL-ST. ELIAS

"Never, before making this trip, have I found myself embosomed in scenery so hopelessly beyond description." JOHN MUIR

Todd Stoeberl
Chief of Interpretation and Education

I've been here for a total of seven years: two years as a district interpreter and five years as chief of interpretation and education. When I was sixteen years old, my family took a vacation to the Black Hills of South Dakota and Yellowstone, and that solidified my desire to be a park ranger.

This place is special to me because of its vast size and the numerous superlatives associated with the park. Wrangell-St. Elias is six times the size of Yellowstone, bigger than Switzerland. It is an incredible resource with big mountains and endless glaciers. It is also the largest designated wilderness in the country.

Located in south-central Alaska; more than 13 million acres
Established December 1, 1978
Official NPS website: www.nps.gov/wrst
- The largest park and preserve managed by the NPS
- The largest single wilderness in the US

My favorite spot? Kennecott has an amazing history; it is a part of the American story. Recently, there has been a reality television show filmed in the park, called *Edge of Alaska*. It is on the Discovery Channel and it has brought quite a bit of publicity to the town of McCarthy, which is near Kennecott.

I love the changing of the colors of fall, and getting ready for winter. This park has over one hundred and twenty miles of coastline. Most visitors have no idea that we are a coastal park. Also, many visitors don't know that we have bison in the park. They are rarely seen but they reside in two herds along a couple of rivers. I spent six years at Theodore Roosevelt National Park, which also has bison, and I have great respect for them.

National parks are places that tell who we are as Americans. Without their protection, our heritage would be lost. National parks are critical to capturing the American identity. They tell the story of America.

Flight on Chitina River
Cindy Grisdela
Reston, Virginia

Twenty years ago, our family began a quest to visit all of the fifty-nine national parks in order to show our two sons the beautiful country we live in. In August 2014 we visited Wrangell-St. Elias, our fiftieth national park visit as a family. This is one of the largest parks in the system, yet there are only sixty miles of roads. Travel is by bush plane, and we spent several wonderful days going on "air safaris" to explore the park. We saw glaciers, went hiking and fishing, and appreciated the beauty of the landscape.

My quilt attempts to capture the memory of being in a small plane, soaring over the rivers, meadows, and streams in the shadow of immense mountains. It was truly a once-in-a-lifetime experience.

Paper Birch

Susan Fernandez
Fairfax Station, Virginia

I am inspired daily by the beauty in nature. It goes well beyond the visual reward. The splendor of the evening sky or a splash of color against an otherwise dull background may be just what I need to recharge after a long day at work.

Paper birch trees and aspen are shade-intolerant trees that can be found at Wrangell-St. Elias.

My first thought when designing the paper birch was how fun it would be to use "paper."

Since real newsprint would not hold up well, I found a newsprint collage fabric print for the main tree. For me, this is where not overthinking the process comes in. The design evolved into a snapshot of the tree trunk with bare branches against the luscious fuchsias of a winter sky. Over-dyed commercial prints from my dye studio along with batiks and pieces of vintage cream and black lace were incorporated into the sky, the branches and the bark. Machine embroidery with variegated and hand-dyed thread added to the bark. A canopy of leaves from other seasons was quilted to the background. The reward is that I am recharged, inspired, and happy.

Boreal Owls

Judy Gula
Annandale, Virginia

Several species of owls are present at Wrangell-St. Elias, including boreal owls.

To make this piece, I used fabric designed with an Indian wooden printing block of an owl. Then I hand stitched it with hand-painted threads from Germany.

Located in Wyoming, Montana, and Idaho; more than 2 million acres
Established March 1, 1872
Official NPS website: www.nps.gov/yell
⬥ Sits atop a massive underground volcano
⬥ The home of Old Faithful and Steamboat Geysers.

YELLOWSTONE

"Every rain-cloud however fleeting, leaves its mark, not only on trees and flowers whose pulses are quickened, and on the replenished streams and lakes, but also on the rocks are its marks engraved whether we can see them or not." JOHN MUIR

Amy Bartlett
Park Spokesperson

I have worked at Yellowstone for twenty-one years in positions ranging from the concessionaire in hotel management, resource management, law enforcement, emergency dispatch, and the public affairs office. Each day offers the possibility of a new adventure, especially with the large and transient population of visitors moving around the park each day. I decided to work for the NPS because I believe places like Yellowstone should be preserved so future generations can enjoy the wonders of this place, as I do. The NPS mission is an honorable one.

Yellowstone has a vast array of amazing sights unparalleled in the United States. It is home to the largest concentration of mammals in the lower forty-eight states. Sixty-seven different mammals reside here, including bison, elk, moose, wolves, wolverines, lynx, and bear. In fact, this is the only place in the US where bison have lived continuously since prehistoric times. The park contains more than 10,000 thermal features, including the world's largest concentration of geysers, as well as hot springs, mudpots, and steam vents. The park also has some unexpected carnivorous plants.

A phenomenal area of the park is the Grand Canyon of the Yellowstone. The depth of the canyon, the roar of the Lower Falls, and intense colors of the canyon walls make it a spot not to be missed! Each season has something wonderful to add. The spring offers a look at the park as new life forms. Dormant plants during the cold grow anew, sending new shoots up through meadows that quickly turn from a soft brown to a vivid green. Bison have their rust colored calves, elk tuck their newly born spotted calves into nooks while they feed, grizzly and black bear are out with their cubs, foraging after a winter of hibernation. While summer is our busiest season, the long warm days encourage exploration of the park's backcountry and provide an easy escape from the summer crowds. Immense wildflowers bloom on hillsides. The bugling of bull elk and appearance of ground cover in hues of orange and red signal the arrival of fall. Fall provides a great view of the rut activity. As snow starts to fall, Yellowstone welcomes the quiet of winter. Winter offers a whole different vision of Yellowstone.

As the nation's first national park, Yellowstone helped instill the need for national parks and played a large role in creating the National Park Service. From the largest concentration of thermal features in the world, to the world's tallest predictable geyser, which is Grand Geyser, to an amazing array of animals and a dedicated group of individuals who work here to protect and preserve the place and ideals of the NPS, this park is an adventure. Every day offers something memorable.

There is an inscription on the Roosevelt Arch at the North Entrance of Yellowstone and it says "For the Benefit and Enjoyment of the People." This is true, for without protection, the animals, landscape, and thermal features would not be here. Animals would be hunted, and thermal features would be tapped for energy. Yellowstone National Park wouldn't be the amazing place it is today where millions come to visit each year.

Grand Canyon of the Yellowstone

Kim K. Gibson
Burke, Virginia

When I was an undergraduate at Guilford College, I was given the opportunity to take a six-week trip across the country in a summer study program. We took the northern route, traveling from North Carolina almost to the West Coast, and back. On July 4, 1976, I stood before Old Faithful in Yellowstone, and was entranced by the power and beauty of the geyser as it soared into the air above me. I fell in love with the park that day. The forces that drive the geyser are well known and mysterious. The size and scale of the hot spot's system were only beginning to be understood then. Though a volcanic caldera with geysers and steam vents, the area contains snow-covered mountains, idyllic lakes, walls of travertine, green valleys, and dense woodlands. It is the essence of wilderness and as the first national park, the ideal of what one should be. I never want to forget that wonderful day.

I would like to thank Kristina MacKaye who beaded the tiny trout in the waterfall of this Yellowstone landscape.

Eveningstar

Deborah A. Dempsey
Oak Hill, Virginia

The rocky slopes of Yellowstone host the eveningstar. At sunset, the enchanting, ten-petaled *Mentzelia decapetala* blazes into full bloom, its intoxicating fragrance drifting under the starry sky.

A hand-painted background was over-dyed with ink to intensify the deep evening colors. This effect was then enhanced with paint sticks for the setting sun, and combined with batik fabric for the stone foundation. The base was free-motion quilted using rayon threads for the ghost leaves and rocky ledge, with hand beading scattered throughout the night sky. The aura of selected constellations is daubed with an iridescent paint stick underneath hand-sewn glass beads. Dimensional overlay began with threads for the grasses. To complete the piece, I used frayed and twisted fabric strips, bonded corduroy, color blocks, satin, grosgrain ribbon fringed and gathered, and silk streaked with colored pencil then finally machine quilted.

Gray Wolf

Jason Wolfson
Chantilly, Virginia

The national parks of our country are great to visit; to honor them was an opportunity I did not want to pass up. This majestic animal is misunderstood yet it has made a wonderful, positive impact on the wildlife in Yellowstone.

My subject matter here comes from a visit to Yellowstone I took back in 2011. I managed to take a picture of a wolf that I spotted in the distance on the side of a hill.

Since I am such novice quilter I rely on the expertise of my wife, Karen, for good advice, even though I can be a terrible student. I am grateful to her for doing the binding, and sleeve and label on the back of this quilt. My mother-in-law, Nancy Adams, also has been helpful, as she is very encouraging of me trying out this timeless art form.

YOSEMITE

> *"Oh these vast, calm, measureless mountain days, inciting at once to work and rest! Days in whose light everything seems equally divine, opening a thousand windows to show us God."* JOHN MUIR

Kari Cobb
Pubic Affairs Specialist

Originally, I wanted to be in the FBI. I came to Yosemite while an undergraduate and I fell in love. A three-day visit became a three-month visit, and I obtained seasonal employment as a ranger. Seasonal work at a national park is a great option for students. Affordable housing is available, you are able to work for your entire summer break, and if it turns out that you love it, rehire opportunities are very good. I have worked here since 2005.

Yosemite is very beautiful. This place offers a lifestyle so important to me. I love the climbing and hiking. This is a fairly small community where you come to know practically everyone. People get along and you can count on your neighbors.

I love exploring, and one of my favorite areas to do that is at Tuolumne Meadows. The topography there is very different than in other parts of the park. It is less busy, many hiking trails begin there, and there are wonderful rounded domes to climb to the top of.

Flexibility at this job allows for nice breaks and walks. Sometimes there are international delegation tours and media productions when I am outside all day. Living in the valley is so nice. My commute to and from my office is about twenty-nine seconds. I live in a 900-square-foot house. It is two and a half hours to the nearest airport.

The valley is only three percent of this park, yet eighty percent of visitors go only there. Other parts of Yosemite have much more to see and are just as beautiful. My advice is to avoid coming on weekends, if your schedule permits. Come early and leave late, and make use of shuttle buses. My favorite flora are not native to the park, but they are the pink dogwood tree and the sugar maple. Pikas are my favorite fauna. They are only found at certain elevations in the park. Although they are shy, they are so cute.

If these lands weren't public, they would be very exclusive clubs. As national parks, they are open and accessible to everyone.

Located in central-eastern California; 761,000+ acres
Established October 1, 1890
Official NPS website: www.nps.gov/yose
- Elevations range from 2,000 to 13,000 feet
- Home to the largest exposed granite monolith in the world, El Capitán

Yosemite National Falls

Kris A. Bishop
Woodbridge, Virginia

This is considered one of the most beautiful and scenic places in the world. Naturalist John Muir once said about Yosemite Falls, "Every rock in its wall seems to glow with life." I was inspired to capture the rock's ruggedness in a bird's eye view of the falls.

Alpine Buttercup

Melinda L. Fuller
Fairfax Station, Virginia

I don't think of myself as artistic, but on consideration, I realize that even though I often use patterns, I almost never use them exactly as designed. In fact, my final product sometimes barely resembles the pattern. To me, a pattern is more a suggestion than a blueprint, and my artistry lies in being able to see beyond the pattern to something I can make on my own.

To date, 1,450 species of wildflowers are documented to reside in Yosemite; one of these is the alpine buttercup. For inspiration, I studied a photo taken by Barry Breckling from a book on California wildflowers.

Bighorn Sheep
Linda H. MacDonald
Powell, Wyoming

When I was younger, I spent many weekends in Yosemite and I hiked the backcountry trails. I was saddened when the Yosemite Sierra Nevada bighorn sheep population nearly died out in the 1990s and I am glad to hear that thanks to their "endangered" listing, their numbers are now recovering. This art quilt is my tribute to the recovery of this subspecies of sheep. The sheer granite cliff on my quilt represents El Capitán.

ZION

"Then came evening, and the somber cliffs were inspired with the ineffable beauty of the alpenglow. A solemn calm fell upon everything." JOHN MUIR

Located in southwestern Utah; 147,000 acres
Established July 31, 1909
Official NPS website: www.nps.gov/zion
▮ Originally known as Mukuntuweap, its name was changed to Zion for fear people wouldn't visit a park if they couldn't pronounce the name

Jin Prugsawan
Park Ranger

I first worked as a volunteer intern with the National Park Service in 2007 at Arlington House: The Robert E. Lee Memorial. I am passionate about history and loved being able to share the stories of Arlington House and Robert E. Lee with the public. The following year I spent a summer working in Yosemite National Park. I spent that summer talking not only about the history of the park but also about the geology, flora, and fauna. I was able to be outdoors and share my knowledge and appreciation for national parks with others; I knew that this was the career for me. I have worked in Zion National Park as a park ranger in the Division of Interpretation since August 2012.

Zion National Park is special to me because each day is different and brings something unique or special to see or experience. The crimson canyon walls and lush green trees that follow the blue and turquoise Virgin River are all mesmerizing. I feel so fortunate to work in such a beautiful national park.

The day of a park ranger can include working at the visitor center orienting new park visitors, helping them plan their trips by suggesting what trails to take, and directing them to different areas to see in the park. Park rangers spend a lot of time hiking on park trails and speaking to park visitors. You may experience a ranger on the trail explaining the geology of a canyon or helping a visitor identify a plant or animal. At other times, rangers lead a wide variety of programs. There is always something new and exciting working as a park ranger in Zion.

My favorite spot in the park is Riverside Walk near the Temple of Sinawava. I have a love for water and feel drawn to it. The Riverside Walk is at the end of Zion Canyon where it becomes the narrowest, where the Virgin River winds through towering Navajo Sandstone walls. The riparian habitat is teeming with life, with rich hanging gardens containing maidenhair ferns, columbine flowers, and Zion shooting stars. There are access points with sandy areas next to the river where you can sit and enjoy the flowing water or appreciate wildlife; where you can see, for example, the American dipper. At the very end of the Riverside Walk, you can peer into the Narrows of the Virgin River, an area where people hike into the river to experience a slot canyon in Zion. It can get so narrow that the towering walls are only twenty feet across in some places. The Riverside Walk is a beautiful area of the park and it is very accessible. It's an easy two-mile round trip walk and a place I love to keep going back to.

I love the spring in Zion; it's a time when the park seems to reawaken. The trees begin to bud and fresh leaves curl open. Wildflowers decorate the trails, and lizards and migratory birds make their appearance. It is a time when the canyon is filled with park visitors and students on spring break, hoping to have their own adventures in Zion.

Although we are in the desert, each summer has a monsoon season. The day might begin blue and sunny without a cloud in the sky, and then in just a few hours the skies can turn black with thunderstorm clouds. Heavy rain can bring flash flooding to slot canyons. This flooding can be dangerous if you are in a slot canyon, like the Narrows, so it is always important to be aware of the weather forecast for the day, realize the flash flood potential, and be cognizant of your surroundings. From a safe position, it is spectacular to see a flash flood in the Virgin River, or to see waterfalls pour over the canyon walls. These events are reminders of how powerful the weather can be: just as deadly as it is beautiful.

One of my favorite birds to see in the park is the peregrine falcon. Each spring after returning from migration, peregrine falcons reclaim some of Zion's towering cliffs. The cliffs below Angels Landing, Cable Mountain, The Great White Throne, and a few others are temporarily closed to climbers while park biologists monitor the birds' nesting activity. Although peregrine falcons have a healthy population today, this majestic bird was at the precipice of extinction when it was declared an endangered species in 1970. Their decline was primarily due to pesticides like DDT, which caused the female to lay thin-shelled eggs that were easily broken, killing the developing embryo inside. Thanks to the US ban on DDT in 1972, as well as the success of captive breeding programs, populations recovered across North America and they were taken off the endangered species list in 1999. Today this amazing predator can be observed spiraling and diving through the blue skies above Zion's crimson canyons. Peregrine falcons are a medium-sized bird with long, pointed wings and a slender tail. Adults are slate gray on their head and back, and they have a black and white barred pattern on their bellies. They have black stripes against their whitish faces resembling sideburns. This aerialist of the sky flies with style, grace, and mesmerizing acrobatics. When hunting, peregrine falcons soar hundreds, even thousands, of feet into the sky. Once it hones in on its prey, typically a smaller bird like a dove or a swallow, the peregrine falcon folds its wings and falls into a nose dive, or stoop, gaining speeds over 200 mph. That's faster than a skydiver freefalling through the sky, making the peregrine the fastest animal in the world. The peregrine then closes its feet, and uses its talons to kill or stun its prey. They are a fascinating bird to see. Zion National Park continues to be an important sanctuary for these falcons and other species.

Memorable events have occurred in Zion, from the ancestral Puebloans whom called Zion home, to the southern Paiute people today who still come to Mukuntuweap, now known as Zion Canyon, to the early Mormon pioneers who farmed the land, to current park visitors who explore the park trails and seek out adventures of their own.

The Narrows

Ricki Selva
Scott Air Force Base, Illinois

You can't simply drive into The Narrows, you must earn them. Exploring this geologic wonder requires bouldering over slick stones, in a torrent of chilly knee- or waist-deep water. Your reward is a slot canyon filled with golden, reflected light.

I dedicate this quilt to two intrepid people who instilled a love of nature, art, and discovery in me and my sister. In spite of a modest budget, my parents made travel our family priority. You can find them memorialized in the quilt as two silhouetted hikers, holding hands as they make their way into the canyon.

As newlyweds, I introduced my husband to Zion in 1980 and we made many trips there over the years. I am grateful to him; he took my vision for this quilt and found a singular perfect image from 1992, from among our tens of thousands of 35mm Kodachrome slides (before digital photography). Thanks also to my sister for locating an image of my parents used for inspiration, taken by me in 1974, which was also buried in a massive collection of family vacation slides. This quilt was constructed from cotton and silk, and embellished with appliqué, piecing, quilting, embroidery, painting, and memories.

Prickly Pear Cactus

Kathy Edwards
Alexandria, Virginia

I begin a piece by thinking of my relation to the work: a memorable location, a family celebration, a childhood memory. In making decisions about my work, I enlarge or decrease the size of my photograph. I make a line drawing of what to include, and resize it. Using photo software, I generate a black and white picture to help determine the light, darks, and medium aspects of the subject. I decide on colors and select the fabrics. I think about texture as I select fabric, threads, and embellishments. I photograph the quilt and re-work it if necessary, until I am satisfied with the results. Then it is declared done.

This piece was inspired by a photo I took while hiking Angel's Landing trail with my husband at Zion. His goal was to reach the summit. My goal was to capture the beauty of the trail as I slowly approached the summit, and I took many pictures. This one addressed the quilt I wanted to make better than the rest. I planned French knots for the cactus, but it was more difficult to plan how to portray the hiking trail. I had to search in my toolbox for threads and paints to depict that trail. I hope you look closer to see the details of my rendering of the prickly pear and yucca plants, and then make plans for your visit to this wonderful park.

Western Spotted Skunk
Gay Bitter
Springfield, Virginia

Skunks aren't spotted, they are striped . . .? This guy is all about his tail, and that's why I chose the spotted skunk, after seeing several photographs of these creatures with their fabulous fluffy tails. The wonderful spotted aboriginal fabric was perfect for creating the spots, and I had fun quilting his tail.

I love the beautiful striations of the rocks of Zion and other western parks, and I tried to capture that in my skunk's landscape. The original composition did not include the flower, but I added it at the last minute, after the quilting was complete. Without a flower, the skunk looked a little lonely, and I wanted a happy skunk!

MORE ABOUT THE NATIONAL PARK SERVICE AND ABOUT THIS PROJECT

"As the only national nonprofit partner to the National Park Service, the National Park Foundation directly supports America's over 400 national parks by pursuing three distinct, yet interdependent, areas of focus: protecting America's national parks through critical conservation and preservation efforts; connecting all Americans with their incomparable natural landscapes, vibrant culture, rich history and the transformative community work of the National Park Service; and inspiring lifelong engagement with the next generation of park stewards."

THE NATIONAL PARKS FOUNDATION

If you are excited about learning more about our national parks, there are many things you can do.

- Read about the parks. Hundreds of books are written about national parks! Find them at the library, your favorite bookstores, or online.

- Visit the parks! Plan carefully, or not; bring your kids and your grandkids and your friends. Take advantage of the many opportunities for all sorts of activities, programs (ranging from photography to sky-watching at night), and hikes designed for varying degrees of fitness and abilities, to name just a few.

- There is a Junior Ranger Program for those aged five to thirteen: www.nps.gov/kids/jrRangers.cfm.

- Volunteer at the parks! Find out more by visiting your local park or check out this website: www.nps.gov/getinvolved/volunteer.htm

- Find out about the Artist-In-Residence Programs: www.nps.gov/subjects/arts/air.htm.

- Explore a career at the parks! Learn about jobs by visiting a park or go to this website: www.nps.gov/aboutus/workwithus.htm.

- Donate to the National Park Service! Find out more by going to this website: www.nps.gov/getinvolved/donate.htm.

One more resource to check out is an exciting project of two brothers, Will and Jim Pattiz, in Atlanta, Georgia. Called More Than Just Parks, it was founded to help raise awareness of our national parks by capturing these national treasures in four- to five-minute short films, and sharing them online. Take a look: www.morethanjustparks.com. (Will and Jim are not employed by the National Park Service.)

Whether or not you are able to visit a national park, if you want to keep informed about goings-on at particular parks, keep in mind that each of the fifty-nine parks has a Facebook page. Look up the park, "like" their page, and you will be treated to a vast number of interesting postings and spectacular images. These Facebook pages are updated regularly and will inspire plenty of daydreams, if not visits.

ARTIST INDEX

Others collect quilts, but DONNA MARCINKOWSKI DESOTO is a collector of quilters. She promotes camaraderie among the unsuspecting with subtle nudges to come have a look, open invitations to join in group quilting challenges, and all-out harangues to drop everything and join in the fun. When not at home with her family in Fairfax, Virginia, she can most often be found in the beloved company of quilters.

DeSoto's artwork has been exhibited at local and national venues, universities, hospitals, healing and charity projects, and in private residences. Her work has been featured in magazines and books, and she is also the author of *Inspired by the Beatles: An Art Quilt Challenge*. She cherishes memories of the many National Parks she has visited. During this second half of her life, she would like to become a National Park volunteer or even a ranger and to be known as a "moose whisperer."

U.S. NATIO

OLYMPIC

NORTH CASCADES

MOUNT RAINIER

GLACIER

WASHINGTON

Columbia River

Missouri River

MONTANA

NORTH DAKOTA

OREGON

IDAHO

Yellowstone River

THEODORE ROOSEVELT

CRATER LAKE

YELLOWSTONE

SOUTH DAKOTA

REDWOOD

Goose Lake

GRAND TETON

WYOMING

WIND CAVE

BADLANDS

LASSEN VOLCANIC

Pyramid Lake

Great Salt Lake

NEBRASKA

North Platte River

NEVADA

Utah Lake

GREAT BASIN

Walker Lake

Mono Lake

UTAH

ROCKY MOUNTAIN

Platte River

YOSEMITE

CALIFORNIA

KINGS CANYON

CAPITOL REEF

ARCHES

COLORADO

PINNACLES

DEATH VALLEY

ZION

BRYCE CANYON

CANYONLANDS

BLACK CANYON OF THE GUNNISON

KANSAS

SEQUOIA

GREAT SAND DUNES

GRAND CANYON

MESA VERDE

Colorado River

CHANNEL ISLANDS

JOSHUA TREE

PETRIFIED FOREST

Salton Sea

ARIZONA

NEW MEXICO

OKLA

Canadian River

PACIFIC OCEAN

SAGUARO

Pecos River

CARLSBAD CAVERNS

GUADALUPE MOUNTAINS

TEXAS

Rio Grande

BIG BEND

ARCTIC OCEAN

CHUKCHI SEA

BEAUFORT SEA

RUSSIA

GATES OF THE ARCTIC

KOBUK VALLEY

BERING STRAIT

Yukon

ALASKA

CANADA

DENALI

WRANGELL-ST. ELIAS

LAKE CLARK

HAWAI'I

NI'IHAU

KAUA'I

O'AHU

BERING SEA

KENAI FJORDS

HONOLULU

MOLOKA'I

HALEAKALĀ

KATMAI

GLACIER BAY

PACIFIC OCEAN

MAUI

GULF OF ALASKA

ALEUTIAN ISLANDS

HAWAI'I

PACIFIC OCEAN

| 0 | 200 | 400 Kilometers |
| 0 | 200 | 400 Miles |

HAWAI'I VOLCANOES